Augmentative and Alternative Communication Systems for Persons with Moderate and Severe Disabilities

Augmentative and Alternative Communication Systems for Persons with Moderate and Severe Disabilities

by

Diane Baumgart, Ph.D.
Associate Professor
Department of Counseling and Special Education
University of Idaho

Jeanne Johnson, Ph.D.
Assistant Professor
Department of Speech and Hearing Sciences
Washington State University

and

Edwin Helmstetter, Ph.D.
Assistant Professor
Department of Counseling Psychology
Washington State University

·P·A·U·L·H·
BROOKES
PUBLISHING Co

Baltimore · London · Toronto · Sydney

Paul H. Brookes Publishing Co.
P.O. Box 10624
Baltimore, Maryland 21285–0624

Typeset by The Composing Room of Michigan, Inc.,
Grand Rapids, Michigan.
Manufactured in the United States of America by
The Maple Press Company, York, Pennsylvania.

Library of Congress Cataloging-in-Publication Data
Baumgart, Diane.
  Augmentative and alternative communication systems for
persons with moderate and severe disabilities / by Diane
Baumgart, Jeanne Johnson, and Edwin Helmstetter.
       p.   cm.
  Includes bibliographical references.
  ISBN 1-55766-049-2 :
  1. Communication devices for the disabled.   I. Johnson,
Jeanne, 1951–   II. Helmstetter, Edwin.   III. Title.
RC429.B38   1990
616.85'503—dc20   90-33268
                                                          CIP

CONTENTS

ACKNOWLEDGMENTS

This text would not have been possible without the expertise, enthusiasm, and support of many people acknowledged hereafter. We would like to take this opportunity to thank them for their contributions.

The text was initially conceptualized during activities supported by Grant G008630162 to the University of Idaho and Grant G00830362 to Washington State University. These two federally funded projects provided many opportunities for the sharing of expertise among practitioners in the field, university students, parents, and the authors. The contributions that these funded activities have created have been tremendous and continue to be seen beyond the funding interval.

There are numerous teachers, related services professionals, parents, special education directors, and classroom aides who have contributed to the design and implementation of the communication systems described in the case histories. We wish to thank Peggy Scuderi, Kathy Schenck, Susan Prudy, John Van Walleghem, Russ Gee, Chris Englehart, Mary Moreau, Carolyn Leavitt, Kathy Stockbridge, Delray Warner, Kathy and Doug Brinkerhoff, Mike Cheresia, Bob West, Jim Christiansen, and Nancy Henderson. Without their professional commitment and expertise, this text would not have been possible. In addition, we wish to thank Margaret Baldwin and Brent A. Askvig for their chapter and section, respectively. We would also like to thank Brent for his assistance in the final stages of manuscript preparation.

The pictures in the text were taken by Charlie Powell and John Van Walleghem. We wish to thank them for their work and the extra efforts they provided during the photo sessions. Jana Schultz did the final typing of the manuscript and her professional skills enabled us to meet timelines and enjoy the writing process. Melissa Behm, Vice President of Paul H. Brookes Publishing Company, provided assistance in the conceptualization and editing of the manuscript. Thank you for that assistance and encouragement.

We wish to thank the persons whose pictures appear throughout the text and their families, and those whose case histories are used as examples. While their identities remain anonymous, as per their wishes, we do acknowledge their contributions to the text. Finally, we wish to thank Myron and Chris for all their support and extra hours of child nurturing, and our friends and family for their understanding and support.

FOREWORD

A "past-present-future" scenario of the development of augmentative and alternative communication systems will examine how far we have come and how far we need to go in providing *every* learner with moderate and severe disabilities a means to express options and choices. Tracing the development of the technology allows us to see how many false starts were made in getting where we are today. A historical perspective also prevents us from being too complacent with the present state-of-the-art strategies. As the technology across a number of diverse fields expands, our knowledge of developing more effective and efficient communication systems has the potential to grow. As professionals, we must keep abreast of developments that can affect a learner's communication system and incorporate those developments into the current knowledge base that is presented in this text.

One of the major drawbacks to developing successful communication interventions 20 years ago was a rather simple one. We did not "look through the eyes of the learner" to determine what might be important to him or her to communicate about, what might make sense in his or her world, what forms he or she already uses to communicate with us, and the reasons for his or her communication attempts. We took bits and pieces from a number of theories and put them into a "model" for intervention. If we step back and look through the eyes of a number of learners form the late 1960s through to 1989, we can see that many of our starts were disjointed . . . sometimes leading nowhere for the learner. And yet, the false starts of placing speech and language skills before communication skills, emphasizing behavioral compliance before expression, implementing nonfunctional programs, and meeting our "agenda" rather than that of the learner, can help us avoid similar mistakes and improve our present knowledge base. A brief historical scenario from the view of Phillip is presented below.

In 1969 Phillip was 3 years old and nonverbal. He was probably thankful that the interventionists did not take the innate theory of language too seriously. If an innate language acquisition device existed in him, it hadn't worked up to that point. He could have told us that normal vocal development has some merit for consideration, but only to a point. The interventionists had learned some important procedures and strategies from the field of applied behavior analysis. They had considered the response they wanted to target, which was speech words. Phillip probably wondered why there was an emphasis on speech and language and not communication. The interventionists had also considered the stimulus conditions under which the response would occur and how Phillip's responses would be consequated. But, did they actually think that using pictures of pants, a woman, and a glass of water to elicit the words "pa," "mama," and "wawa," and consequating Phillip's imitation of those words with popcorn and soda would, in any way, present a functional relationship to Phillip? After 2 years of learning to say three words, he could put his own pants on, but asking for them was not a priority on his list of communication messages. He was a ward of the state, and, therefore, had no need to call or refer to his mother. Now the word "water" might be useful to request a drink, but Phillip couldn't quite make the generalization from the picture of a glass to the water fountain in his living environment. What Phillip really wanted was the popcorn and soda. He'd play their game and say "mama" to get the popcorn. Why they didn't just teach "popcorn" was beyond him. Some of Phillip's peers were learning 100 different ways to request candy. He's seen the interventionist hold up pictures of a cup, ball, car, and so on, and ask, "What's this?" When his friend Roy would answer, he'd get candy. Phillip thought it was unusual that both he and Roy always had to be sitting with both feet on the floor and both hands in their lap to be able to say their words. The interventionists called it "maintaining attention." Why did his teachers and other adults talk when they were standing or walking or doing 100 other things? Phillip did notice when his friend Roy said, "be.....aaa....l" on the playground, that no one understood he wanted the "ball." But then Roy usually received the ball when he pointed to it so maybe saying the word wasn't too important anyway.

Phillip felt that the interaction that made absolutely no sense at all (but then it wasn't a real interaction) was this thing the interventionists call "object identification." Three objects were placed in front of him (at least they used the real objects this time) and the interventionist would say, "Give me the cup." When he would give it to her, she didn't use it, or even give him juice in the cup; she put it right back or moved it around as in a shell game . . . something called randomization. He couldn't understand why he always had to give it to her; she could reach it just as well as he could. But, he did get popcorn when he did it.

Other friends of Phillip were having a more difficult time learning speech words. The interventionists spent so much time teaching them to imitate patting their stomachs and their heads, and pounding the table. But these friends couldn't learn to say sounds with these funny actions. The interventionists were so set on teaching this that they missed it when Phillip's friend, Julie, pointed to the cheese and gestured "eat." It took a few years for the interventionists to come to the conclusion that if Julie could imitate patting her stomach and other non-functional gestures, then she could probably learn manual sign language. Phillip was proud of the way Julie could use signs. However, it was too bad that no one taught the teachers or the parents what they meant. Julie became frustrated when she couldn't get people to respond to her signs. But, she could get their attention when she hit her head . . . that always worked to bring someone over.

As the years went by, the interventionists were doing something new. They were now asking the classroom teachers what words and signs were important for the learners to use. And what words did Phillip's teacher choose? Boring words like "bathroom" and "sit." Wouldn't it have been wonderful if they would have noticed that he and his friends liked to go to the store, spend money, and buy things like gum, soda, and potato chips. Isn't that what most teenage boys like? Actually, Phillip could go to the bathroom by himself, but his friend Roy had no intentions of asking to go to the bathroom. If the teachers thought that teaching Julie the sign for bathroom was going to solve her toileting program problems, they were in for a big shock.

Julie did learn many signs and gradually the teachers began to use them in the classroom. Other of Phillip's friends were having a more difficult time. One learned to sign "eat" and hadn't learned any other signs in 2 years. Another friend, Joe, had learned three signs and used them all each time someone asked, "What do you want?" Joe just couldn't figure out which signs stood for what. It didn't please the teacher when Joe always imitated the last sign in the teacher's sentence each time she asked a question, made a request, or told him he did a good job. Actually, Phillip thought Joe was pretty smart. If he didn't know what the teacher's message was, he at least stayed in the conversation by imitating back to her. Joe just couldn't understand the intent of the teacher's message, but he tried to do *something* to please him.

When Phillip and his friends went to live in the community, he could see that it opened up a whole new set of things to talk or sign about. There were so many choices that could be made if anyone took the time to ask. They did get to go to the fast food restaurants. He did feel sorry for Kim, however, because even though her communication board helped her express herself, the teacher made her point to the word, "yes" on her board when the cashier asked if she wanted french fries. The cashier understood her head nod. But her teacher said she had to use her "system" of communication. It took her so long to move her hand to the right-hand corner of the board where "yes" was located. And the people waiting in line were getting a little impatient. What's so wrong with just letting Kim nod her head "yes"? Everyone understands that. Phillip saw Kim get frustrated. When she wanted to communicate with someone, she had no way to get their attention. She always had to wait until an adult came over to her, and they never used her communication board. They talked to her and she had to point to pictures. If she would have had some other words on her board, she would have been able to tell them a thing or two.

Finally, the interventionists and teachers learned that young infants learn to communicate **before** they learn to say their first words and that there are many different reasons to communicate. Phillip thought that this had wonderful implications for helping some of his friends who had more severe disabilities than him . . . friends who didn't have enough motor control to use signs, or who couldn't understand or see pictures. Phillip knew that when Mary tensed her body and made a face that she didn't like what was happening. She could also use some body movements to indicate that she did like something. These behaviors communicated to Phillip. How long would it take for the interventionists and teachers to- "read" these signals as Mary's form of communication? Now, they could have asked Mary's parents and they could have told the staff how Mary communicated, but there didn't seem to be very good communication between the home and the school. It was too bad that Mary wasn't "eligible" for programs in the area of speech, language, and communication. Phillip heard them say that she didn't have the prerequisites and some funny thing about her cognitive level. They apparently didn't see Mary use her eyes to indicate that she did know what was going on in her world. It probably didn't help that Mary also couldn't hear very well, so she couldn't understand what the adults were saying to her. Did Phillip really hear them right? Did someone say that Mary couldn't benefit from hearing aids because of her level of functioning? Phillip noticed that Mary was left alone more and more of the time. She used to smile a lot when someone came up to her. She wasn't smiling much anymore since very few adults interacted with her. Last year Mary's teacher gave her a calling device that she could use if she was positioned just right. Wow, this was great for Mary. Mary loved to push it and get the teacher's attention. Phillip wondered what happened to the device and why the new teacher didn't use it or didn't order another one. Plus, Mary was getting confused. Her parents would make one gesture when they would get her up, the teacher would make another, and the physical therapist would just pick Mary up and put her on the big ball without gesturing or saying a word. Mary always wondered where she was going and what was about to happen.

Now Phillip is 23 years old. He thinks that he was one of the lucky ones. He did learn to talk even though most people can only understand him if they know him really well or if he pairs his speech with many gestures. He has also learned to be fairly independent so he can do things for himself. Therefore, there isn't a lot to talk about as he gets older. He has to tell the adults where he is going, but no one ever asks if he liked the movie or if he would rather have a different job. No one at work can understand him so they don't bother to talk to him much anymore. And going to the grocery store is a real problem. It takes so long for him to let the people who work there know what he wants when he can't find an item.

The assumptions and strategies outlined in this text may have made sense to Phillip years ago. Concepts such as chronological age—appropriate content and materials, functionality, quality social interactions among many different persons, zero exclusion, social significance, the use of multiple systems to get a message across, and being taught in the natural environment would have improved the quality of life for Phillip and his friends. If Phillip could adequately express his wishes today, what might they be? Perhaps he might tell us that one of the major ways that his friends are denied the freedom to make choices and to have options is by their lack of opportunities for normalized experiences in the school, home, workplace, and community. Many states and local school districts denied learners, such as his friend Mary, communication services in the year 1989. Until: 1) the service of "speech and language" is broadened to include "communication" as a critical related service and 2) all teachers and related service personnel are taught that behaviors communicate and that no learner is so profoundly disabled that he or she can't benefit from augmentative and alternative programs, many learners younger than Phillip will be considered ineligible for communication intervention services.

If Phillip could have a "wish list" for the future, his list might read as follows:

1. That no learner, regardless of the severity of his or her disability, be denied a more effective and efficient means of communicating
2. That augmentative and alternative systems, which have been developed and are effective, not get lost because of poor transition planning
3. That an emphasis on nonsymbolic receptive communication and the learner's understanding of the many functions of communication addressed to him or her be made (for successful interactions to occur, the message must be repaired if it breaks down in either direction)
4. That an integrated team approach of teachers, speech-language pathologists, occupational and physical therapists, and parents be utilized with each learner to develop an augmentative or alternative communication system
5. That each person or team responsible for developing an augmentative system for an individual learner consider the points made in the following text: before new systems are developed for an individual, the learner's existing forms and functions must be recognized.

This text offers a wealth of information to "get started" and to expand a learner's current system of communication. It points out that there will be some false starts; we cannot let these interfere with asking new questions and moving on. In the future, it is hoped, Phillip can look back and say, "I can't believe they didn't know that in 1989." New developments in technology and the federal funding of statewide assistant device resource centers have exciting implications to expand the present state-of-the-art practices and strategies that are described in this book. Perhaps Phillip's historical perspective and the case histories presented in this text will provide the reader with examples of the use of the theoretical information that is available.

Kathleen Stremel, M·A·
Senior Researcher
University of Southern Mississippi

INTRODUCTION

This text was written to assist professionals and parents involved in developing augmentative or alternative communication systems for individuals with moderate and severe disabilities who also are nonverbal. There are many excellent texts, research articles, and position papers that provide theoretical and philosophical support and information on enhancing and developing systems for children, youth, and adults with moderate and severe disabilities. However, numerous requests have been made for examples of the use of the theoretical information. This text is a response to those requests and provides guidelines and exemplars for "getting started."

This text also was written as an affirmation of the capability of all individuals to communicate. In the past, some professionals believed that persons with moderate or severe disabilities could be excluded from educational or related services designed to enhance alternative or augmentative communication. The rationales that were provided varied. In the case of *Timothy W. vs. Rochester School District* (Staff, 1989), the rationale that was provided was that Timothy "was not capable of benefiting" from services and thus was excluded from both educational and related services (p. 2). The court determined that the issue was not whether services should be provided, but rather "what constitutes an appropriate education program" (p. 2). Thus, it is hoped that this text can assist teachers, related service personnel, administrators, and parents to design and implement appropriate communication programs.

A number of assumptions have been made regarding the background of the reader of the text; therefore, a brief explanation of the field terminology that has been used is included in this introduction to enable the reader to more clearly understand the text and locate the information it contains.

The process of selecting, designing, and using a communication system requires a synthesis of knowledge and expertise from many disciplines. It is assumed that the reader has a working knowledge of these areas and will refer to the resources listed at the end of Chapter Five and in the references for additional information. It is also assumed that the reader has the background in applied behavior analysis and measurement strategies necessary to design and implement instructional programs and to evaluate the outcomes. Examples of assessment procedures and data collection forms are contained in the chapters containing the case histories and in the Appendix.

The term communication system has been used in the text to refer to systems designed to enhance verbal speech and to be used when verbal speech is not used. These types of systems are commonly referred to as augmentative communication systems and alternative communication systems, respectively. In some examples and in the case histories, communication systems were designed to augment verbal speech, and in others they were designed as an alternative system. The term communication system is used in the text, and refers to both augmentative and alternative communication systems.

In summary, the text provides assumptions and factors to consider prior to selecting and designing a system, guidelines and steps to assist in getting started with the selection and design process, some specific assessment procedures, and actual case histories where systems were designed and used. Although the names in the case histories have been changed and references to actual places altered, the information presented is based upon actual cases. Regardless of the age of the person, handicapping condition, and previous history, if the individual is observed, listened to and provided adequate time to respond, the messages he or she is sending will be "heard."

REFERENCES

Staff. (1989, August). Victory for Timothy W. *TASH Newsletter*, 15(8), p. 1. (Can be obtained from The Association for Persons with Severe Handicaps, 7010 Roosevelt Way, N.E., Seattle, WA 98115.)

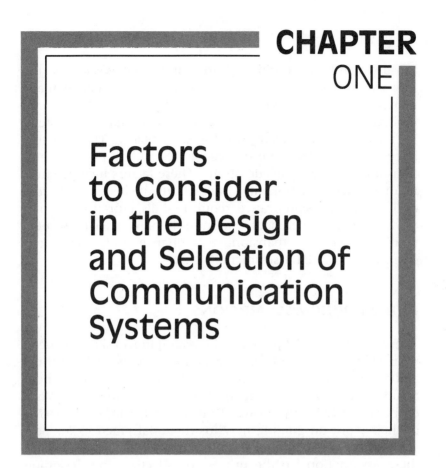

CHAPTER
ONE

Factors to Consider in the Design and Selection of Communication Systems

Prior to selecting and designing any communication system, a number of factors should be systematically considered. Too often, in the excitement of implementing a system, critical factors are overlooked, resulting in the system actually limiting rather than enhancing communication options. There are numerous other examples in which the best intentions in the design and selection did not produce the anticipated favorable results. For instance, an abstract symbol system that was designed for a 5-year-old girl seemed to be the perfect communication system for use with her teachers but was unusable with other young children. Similarly, consider the case in which a wooden tray with seven pictures was attached to a wheelchair and used during classroom sessions; however, in the cafeteria, the food obscured the pictures and the tray was

1

too awkward to reposition. Furthermore, on weekends, the tray was stored in the closet by the parents because it made maneuvering in the house too difficult. To avoid unforeseen limitations in the design and use of a communication system, 15 factors are described and discussed below. These factors have been organized into two categories: philosophic assumptions and practical considerations. These factors include chronological age, functionality, interactions, inclusion with zero exclusion, social significance, requisite skills, pluralism, natural environment, preferences, parent–school partnerships, portability, audience, expansion, maintenance, and comprehensive and integrated assessment.

PHILOSOPHIC ASSUMPTIONS

There are at least 10 philosophic assumptions that have been utilized in the design of communication systems by the authors and are evident in the case histories that follow. Many of these assumptions have been identified and described by Wolfensberger (1972) and Brown, Branston-McLean, et al. (1979) in their work on guiding new instructional practices for persons with severe disabilities. Because of the importance of these assumptions to the process of selecting and designing augmentative systems, they will be reiterated with emphasis placed upon their relevance to communication.

Chronological Age

Consideration of the chronological age factor should lead the instructional team to select vocabulary and a system that will enable the person to participate in activities and to communicate with his or her peers regarding choices, preferences, or messages that are appropriate for someone of the same chronological age. The mental ages of the person can and will come into consideration when deciding how to instruct (e.g., types and complexity of prompts), but not in the process of determining objects, people, environments, or activities in which communication and, thus, instruction will occur. If a sandbox is used during recess by children in second grade, then sandboxes might be a vocabulary word of a child with disabilities of the same age. This would not be considered chronologically age-appropriate for the same child if he or she were in junior high, unless nondisabled-age peers frequently used a sandbox. Vocabulary and types of representations can reflect chronological age if, and only if, the curriculum for the student and the goals, objectives, instructional settings, and materials reflect this philosophy.

Functionality

For more than a decade, functionality of an instructional objective has been a guiding factor in the design and selection of curricula for persons with moderate or severe disabilities. Brown and his colleagues (Brown, Branston, et al., 1979; Brown, Branston-McLean, et al., 1979) have defined functionality as actions that, if not performed by a student with disabilities, would have to be performed by someone else for him or her. This definition can be applied to the process of selecting the content (i.e., vocabulary) of the communication system. If the system or its content allows the person to indicate or say something that, if not said by the person, would have to be said by someone else, then that content should be considered for inclusion within the augmentative communication system. For example, if a student doesn't ask for a second helping of lunch in the high school cafeteria, either he or she will not receive more or someone else will need to make the request. Within the routine of the day, choices are often made for nonverbal people because they lack the means to state their choice. Too often this can result in a lack of choices being offered to the person with the disability. It is critical, then, to use the routine of the day and those activities typically performed by nondisabled peers to highlight times when choices are available or could be offered and to consider the functionality of stating a choice, preference, or other message during those events. Inherent within this process is a selection of activities to perform and related instructional goals that have already been determined to be functional in nature.

Interactions

The definition of communication and language (i.e., one person sending a message by some means to another person, for a reason, in a certain setting) could be the definition of language and communication as long as it is understood that the means used to send messages are quite different. Language uses symbolic forms (e.g., words) and requires formal rules for formation and translation, while communication uses nonsymbolic forms (e.g., gestures, body postures) with informal, mutually understood conventions used for sending and receiving messages. Germane to both communication systems is a sender and a receiver of the messages. Thus, in all instances, it is critical that the user of an augmentative system have opportunities to both send and receive messages and that the settings provide this opportunity with a variety of peers, not just instructional personnel or classmates. These opportunities for interactions are critical to communication. Limiting the interactors has the effect of limiting the reasons for interacting as well as the messages. Data collected on the interactions between pupils and teachers indicate that the majority of messages sent by teachers are requests or demands that require limited communication from students. Thus, other partners such as classmates, peers, and familiar and unfamiliar adults in a variety of settings are vital to communication.

Inclusion with Zero Exclusion

The history of special education and speech and language therapy is filled with examples of changing criteria regarding who can benefit from instruction, with each field becoming more and more inclusive. A large part of this can be attributed to an improved technology of teaching and to changes in attitudes that have allowed people formerly excluded from education to receive instruction. This philosophy, one of inclusion without exclusion, is advocated here. Typically, assessment procedures were used to determine if a person was a candidate for a formal language communication system. Unfortunately, these criteria resulted in the exclusion of numerous students from any form of language or communication intervention. Typically excluded were children, youth, or adults with the characteristics and for the reasons that follow:

1. Those with aggressive behaviors or other behavior problems. It was postulated that the behaviors should be reduced or eliminated and compliance obtained prior to any language or communication intervention.
2. Those who did not consistently indicate desires or wants to others. It was thought that such persons did not have the cognitive ability to indicate these messages and, thus, would not benefit from intervention.
3. Those who did not score on cognitive scales as having attained the level of Sensorimotor Stage VI. It was postulated that these persons were not ready yet for language and the skills involved would be too difficult and frustrating for them. Unfortunately, these students were excluded from the interactions that language usage facilitates and from instruction to enhance communication.
4. Those who, even with a communication system, would not be able to independently use it to communicate. It was thought that instruction must result in independent performance in order to be considered beneficial or worthwhile. If mental, behavioral, or motoric difficulties precluded independence, these students were not offered systems for communication.
5. Those with sensory impairments who could not reliably indicate intentionality of actions or those whose response forms varied from person to person. It was postulated that consistent responses were necessary prerequisites to initiating any language or communication intervention.

The position of the authors is that exclusionary practices are history. Research indicates that children, youth, and adults with some or all of these characteristics can benefit from intervention and must be provided instruction in the use of non-symbolic and symbolic communication. In addition, service providers must receive instruction to enable them to reinterpret behavioral actions as a form of communication, and to assist peers and others in the community to recognize nonsymbolic and symbolic communication messages.

Social Significance

Although important gains have been made to alter the "stereotypes" with which those with disabilities are portrayed, certain ones still remain. Consideration of the social significance factor in the design and use of the augmentative communication system can help assure that the social significance of the person using the system is enhanced as much as possible. This factor plays an important role not only in the selection of referents for a system, but also in the manner in which it is transported, the assistance provided to use it, and the interactions for which it is used. For example, take the following two systems, both designed to enhance the communication of a person with visual impairments and moderate mental disabilities. One system was a felt apron that the person wore around his waist. Attached to the apron were a white doll shoe, pink doll glass, and a preschool toy car, ideally picked to represent gym class, drink, and time to ride on the bus, respectively . The second system was a black cloth audio tape holder that the person carried or attached with Velcro to a belt. The miniatures were a doll-sized Nike basketball shoe, a drinking mug, and a toy van replica that represented the same vocabulary as the first system. In addition, when using the first system to order a beverage in a restaurant, the first person pointed to the cup and had a beverage ordered for him by his teacher. With the second system, the person was asked if he wanted a beverage and was then taught to place his own order. Given that each person was eighteen, it seems obvious that the first system was not only chronologically age-inappropriate, but also did not enhance the perceived social standing of the person using the system. It is this last point, enhancing perceived social standing, that should result. This can occur not only by ensuring that the factors discussed above are considered but also by ensuring that the norms for what is perceived as important or significant in the environment are determined and used in the formative evaluation of the system. This formative evaluation should involve peers and should address the individual's gestures, vocabulary, and opportunities to communicate and interact that are currently in vogue at that particular time in the community. In some cases, especially with adolescents and adults, this factor may be more significant than cognitive ability or developmental readiness in the selection of a symbolic versus a nonsymbolic system. Thus, in spite of the fact that an actual shoe may be more concrete to a person when requesting a bowling shoe, the social significance factor would suggest that a miniature shoe or a photo of a shoe might be used instead.

Requisite Skills

The process of communicating typically involves numerous skills in addition to forming a sign or pointing to a photo to greet someone. The position of the authors is that the process of interacting is so critical that it should remain the focus of the instruction. Other skills should be taught concurrently or adaptations should be used so that a lack of skills does not interfere with opportunities to interact and communicate. Skills should not be deemed to be prerequisites to communication and taught prior to enhancing or increasing opportunities for interactions and communication. For instance, a young child or an adult may not have the skills to open a communication booklet, hold it open, and point to a page without blocking the picture on that page. Certainly these skills can be practiced in an instructional setting. But, at the same time, the booklet can be opened for the person and held while he or she is assisted to point, or the process can be adapted by removing a page, teaching and instructing the person to either put it down on a counter when ordering or to hand the page to another person and receive it back when the message has been understood. The exact instructional procedure and associated goals and objectives will vary considerably from person to person, but the requirement that the skills needed to use the system be in the repertoire of a person prior to obtaining or using a specific system should not differ.

Pluralism

Pluralism, or the use of more than one type of system, seemingly contradicts what many parents and other professionals see as the goal of the communication system assessment process. That is, many professionals have assumed that the assessment process should result in the design and selection of one system. Reflection on the communication modes used by those who are verbal may illustrate the limitations imposed if only one system is available. Imagine for a minute a teacher who is also a wife and mother of an infant. Her communication with her infant consists primarily of facial expressions accompanied by coo and ah sounds that her infant responds to enthusiastically. A total change in verbalizations and gestures is used when she lectures. Likewise, a written note left for her husband is a third and efficient form of communication to remind him to pick up the kids since she is teaching tonight. In each instance, the form for sending a message was selected to meet the needs of a different audience. This same flexibility and combination of gestures and other forms must be available to users of communication systems.

For many persons with severe disabilities, the form or system selected will be different as the audience changes. At times, the communication system may match the abilities of the targeted audience more than the abilities of the sender. For example, John, age 6, uses gaze and reaching toward a pitcher at the dinner table to indicate a request for a drink. This form is also acknowledged by staff at school, the after school program, and the Special Olympics activities. However, to order a drink in a restaurant, John uses a photo of a beverage with the message, "A small orange drink, please," written on it. This second form was selected because the first form was not readily understood or useable by restaurant personnel and because the latter form enhanced John's social standing in these situations. Thus, John has two forms, one selected because it matches his abilities and is useable in many settings and one that matches the abilities of clerks in restaurants. Although it is preferable to select one communication system, hopefully one that matches the cognitive abilities of the user, one system does not always meet the existing myriad of communication needs. When the discrepancy in cognitive abilities between the sender and the audience is large, as in the cases of John and restaurant personnel and the teacher and her infant, it is likely that more than one system will be required.

Natural Environment

It is difficult to imagine engaging in a variety of activities with different people in various settings throughout the day and not having a means to communicate. It is because of those typical opportunities to communicate that optimal instructional environments for enhancing communication are the natural environments and routines within the day. Blocking off a time interval to "teach language, communication, or interaction skills" is justified only when this instruction is in addition to that which is already provided within naturally occurring routines and interactions with peers. It is sometimes necessary, and, in fact, desirable, to practice skills that are difficult to perform, or to role play interactions in order to become more proficient. These, along with other instructional practices, can enhance communication, but should always be in addition to providing instructional and/or structured opportunities in the natural environment.

Preferences

Inevitably teachers, parents, and other adults have vocabulary and/or intents that they wish to have included in a communication system. Usually these include a symbol for bathroom, drink, and some leisure activity that the person can do independently. Although some or all of these may be included in a communication system, the primary determinant of the communication should be the person using the system. Thus, the initial symbols should represent messages that an assessment process has determined are already being sent. This allows the student to "say" something that he or she is already motivated to say, learn a minimal number of new skills, and more readily be understood. A typical problem that arises when using preferences is that the most frequent message is "no," and it is interpreted as noncompliance, or the person is not seen as communicating anything. Both of these issues, as well as others, are discussed more extensively in Chapters Two and Three. The solutions, in each instance, should be to select initial communication that is already within the repertoire in some form (e.g., gesture only, intent and gesture) and to allow the person to use a new, more readily understood form to express the same function and power of communication.

Parent-School Partnerships

There is general agreement among professionals and data from researchers that when caregivers and school personnel both teach and/or reinforce the same behavior, learning is faster and generalization and maintenance of skills is more likely. Conflict often arises, however, when either the caregivers or school personnel do not provide opportunities or encouragement to use a communication system. There is little basis for school personnel to not implement a communication system when it is at a parent's or caregiver's request. However, when school personnel implement a communication system and the opportunities to use it occur or are encouraged only at school, concerns regarding continued use of the system arise. In this situation, some teachers opt to wait to implement the system at school until the caregivers agree to teach or use the system at home. Other teachers start instruction and limit input or contact with caregivers who are viewed as "not involved anyway." Finally, some teachers proceed with instruction, continue to communicate with caregivers, and seek their input and evaluations. It is this last scenario that the authors support and encourage. Given that the caregivers had opportunities for significant input into the system and it could facilitate communication in the home setting, the hesitation or refusal to use the system at home should not be a barrier to implementation at school. The experience of the authors is that very often school personnel place an expectation on caregivers to "teach" the use of the communication system. Some caregivers may be hesitant to take on the role of teacher. This behavior is interpreted as a lack of commitment or involvement. Implementation at school, continued positive contact with caregivers, and demonstrated success at school are often the supports needed in order for the system to be used (not taught) at home.

PRACTICAL CONSIDERATIONS

Using an augmentative system can be made easier and proceed more smoothly if factors that relate to daily use are considered prior to the final design and selection of the communication system. Consideration of at least the factors of portability, audience, adaptability, expansion, and maintenance will enhance the probability that the system, once completed, will serve the needs of the user across most situations, with a variety of people, in the most accommodating fashion. A number of questions are listed below to assist in the process of choosing an augmentative system. Addressing these questions prior to the design and selection of the system will help those that are involved to achieve the most desirable result with minimal oversights. It is important that caregivers, teachers, and related service professionals be involved in reviewing the questions to ensure that the final product maximizes communication with familiar as well as unfamiliar age peers and others.

Portability

Portability refers to the ease with which the communication system can be readily moved and/or carried. Since voice and hands are usually "built in," using these means to communicate are rated as the most portable. If a system external to these means is used, it is more of a burden to move and transport. A goal in designing and selecting a system that is external to the body is to minimize this burden. The following questions can assist in this goal:

1. Is there a way to transport the system besides holding it, such as:
    a. Attaching it to a wheelchair?
    b. Carrying it in a backpack, purse, wallet, pocket, note-book, waist pack, or similar belt purse?
    c. Attaching it to a belt?
    d. Having someone else carry it?
2. Can the size and weight of the system be limited? Some possibilities may be:
    a. Containing the system in a 3 inch by 5 inch or 5 inch by 7 inch holder initially?
    b. Removing and adding items initially so that all vocab-ulary does not have to be carried to all places?

Audience

Audience refers to the people with whom the user will send and receive messages. Consider the following points to ensure that the communication system(s) that was selected uses means that are readily understood:

1. Will adults both familiar and unfamiliar with the system readily understand the specific meaning of the message? Would written words attached in some way on the symbol help with comprehension?
2. Will same-age peers, both familiar and unfamiliar with the system, understand the messages that are sent? For non-reading children, is there someone nearby to interpret the messages to them? Is it possible to provide awareness training to children who have frequent opportunities to interact with these communication system users?
3. Will one system using one or more types of representations

meet the needs of the audience? Are different systems needed for different audiences?

4. Is the system usable by others to send messages, paired with words, to the person with a disability? Would this enhance comprehension? What is needed to enable this to occur?

Expansion

Expanding the communication system should necessitate a totally new planning process. Concerns that address this issue include:

1. Can the layout and organization of the system facilitate larger utterances?
2. Are the symbols that are selected for use readily available? Could a combination of types of representations be used such as photos, line drawings, commercial pictures, and miniatures to enhance availability?
3. Will expansion substantially increase the bulk of the system and hinder its portability? If so, could vocabulary for specific environments be kept in a stationary place and added and selected as appropriate?
4. What procedures are in place to ensure continued input from the family, the user, and others into the expansion of the system?
5. What evaluation system will be used to determine the current success and problems with the communication system as well as future needs for expansion?
6. Who has the primary responsibility for expanding the communication system?

Maintenance

After a communication system has been constructed, procedures and responsible personnel should be identified for ensuring that it remains in good condition. Systems used during meals and breaks typically require cleaning after each use.

Likewise, their use during recess, community outings, and transporting can result in wear and, thus, necessary repair. Answering the following questions can help to ensure that the communication system will remain in good condition.

1. What routines for cleaning and grooming does the individual use? Can cleaning the communication system be incorporated into any of these routines?
2. Are there additional materials that are needed to clean the system? What are they and where can they be stored for ready access?
3. Are there additional representations (e.g., miniatures) and holders readily available so that the system can be repaired as needed?
4. Who will take primary responsibility for cleaning and repairing the system? How will the user be involved in these activities?

Comprehensive and Integrated Assessment

In order for a system to enhance communication between sender and listener, the skills of both as well as environmental factors must be assessed and integrated into all aspects of its use. It is common to find that skills needed to use a communication system have not been previously assessed (e.g., a standardized fine motor assessment was conducted but did not state which 3 inch by 5 inch area in an opened notebook the person could point to quickly and accurately). It is beyond the scope of this section to discuss each of the skill areas in depth. A listing of sources for assessment procedures and information and procedures on the assessment of: tracking and scanning, hand preference, and basic receptive language skills have been provided at the end of Chapter Five. Questions to review prior to conducting a comprehensive assessment are listed below:

1. Have professionals with expertise in physical therapy, occupational therapy, speech and language therapy, special education, vision and hearing, and mobility been contacted and assessments scheduled?

2. Have the results of the motor and vision assessments been translated into how the skills can be used with different sized objects or pictures, in various layouts, and with different referents?
3. Have the results of the language, cognitive, and behavioral assessments been translated into the functions (e.g., meanings, intents) and forms (e.g., signals, responses) used for communications, as well as the degree of abstraction the person comprehends?
4. Has one professional (e.g., teacher, parent) been assigned the role of case manager?
5. Have timelines for conducting the assessments and summarizing the results been determined?

SUMMARY

This chapter contains a list of ten philosophic and five practical considerations to assist in the design and implementation of a communication system. Careful and systematic review of these considerations can help interventionists avoid the many false starts that are discussed in the foreword through the eyes of Phillip. They can be used not only in the planning stages but also in the evaluation stages to determine if the system "works" for the individual, the communication partners, the caregivers, throughout the many environments in which messages are exchanged. These considerations are fundamental to the systems described in the case histories as well as to the information on behavior as communication, and getting started with a system covered in the next chapters.

CHAPTER
TWO

Treating
Problem
Behaviors
as Communication

A significant proportion of persons with moderate or severe disabilities also display behavior problems. These behaviors, also referred to as "aberrant," "inappropriate," or "excessive" behaviors, include self-abuse, aggression toward the environment or other persons, repetitive vocalizations or motor behavior, unusual oral behavior (e.g., pica, rumination), and disruptive behavior (e.g., screaming, tantrums). Some problem behaviors threaten the health of the individual or others in the environment, interfere with learning adaptive behavior, or disrupt social interactions. Treatment has often focused on the reduction of the problem behavior and the strengthening of an alternative, appropriate response. In most cases, the methods used to reduce the behavior and the response that was

17

strengthened were designed without any analysis of the purpose of the problem behavior.

The numerous issues that surround the behavior-reduction approach include: 1) if behavior change is desirable in the presence of different persons and in multiple settings, then some degree of treatment must be provided in some or all of these situations; 2) treatment may need to be reinstated periodically if long-term behavior reduction is desired; 3) it is extremely difficult, if not impossible, to predict and control unwanted side effects, such as aggression or self-injury; and 4) without analysis of the purpose of performing the behavior other problem behaviors may emerge to fill a similar purpose. Recently, other questions have been raised about the use of interventions that devalue the person being treated, the inappropriateness of certain practices for community and other integrated settings, the failure of the behavior-reduction approach to significantly improve the quality of the individual's life, and the failure to link treatment strategies to the individual's need to communicate.

As a result of the issues raised above, different approaches have emerged as alternatives to the behavior-reduction methods. The approach described here utilizes a process that involves analyzing the cause and purpose of the behavior, generating and testing hypotheses about the cause and purpose of behavior, and using those results to develop and implement treatments (Donnellan, Mirenda, Mesaros, & Fassbender, 1984; Evans & Meyer, 1985; Meyer & Evans, 1989). The steps of this process are described below.

INTERVENTION AND
BEHAVIOR PROBLEMS: AN OVERVIEW

Analysis: Questions to Ask

In some cases, it is possible to gain an understanding of problem behavior by speaking with the individual who is displaying the behavior. With an understanding of why an individual engages in problem behavior, practitioners are more likely to design successful interventions. When communication is impaired, however, as is the case with many persons who have moderate or severe disabilities, understanding the individual's behavior can become extremely difficult without a systematic plan for analyzing it. To adequately analyze the problem behaviors of persons with moderate or severe disabilities, it is important that parents and professionals address the right questions. Questions to address during the analysis stage are listed below. The list of questions, while not exhaustive, addresses many different aspects of the individual's life.

Question 1: Is There a Possible Medical Reason for the Behavior? Certain diseases and syndromes are associated with self-injury (e.g., Lesch-Nyhan disease, Cornelia de Lange syndrome) and repetitive behavior (e.g., Rett syndrome). Certain medications, such as those used for controlling seizures, aggression, and activity level, can have side effects that might be interpreted as behavior problems. Allergies can cause restlessness, rubbing and scratching, irritability, and lethargy. Diet can affect alertness and motivation. Seizure activity can include inattentiveness, aggressive or disruptive behavior, self-injury, and repetitive vocal or motor behavior. Pain can cause aggression, self-injury, inattentiveness, and changes in activity level. Sensory impairments can cause individuals to engage in unusual behaviors in order to avoid tasks involving the impaired sensory modality. Thyroid gland problems can lead to major behavioral changes such as lethargy, anxiety, and psychotic behavior.

This is neither an exhaustive list of examples, nor a guide for use in identifying possible medical causes of behavior. Individuals react differently to specific causes, and so a list of behavioral responses to medical causes cannot be relied upon. The examples do, however, highlight the significant role that medical factors can play, and emphasize the need to always consider their role. Health professionals or the parents must be contacted if a medical problem could or does exist. The reader is referred to other sources for information about medical conditions (Batshaw & Perret, 1986; Blackman, 1984; Gadow,

1986; Haslam & Valletutti, 1985; Holvoet & Helmstetter, 1989).

Question 2: Is the Problem Related to the Social Environment? When the behavior occurs, note the staff and peers who are and are not present, the size and composition of the social environment, the amount and type of interactions, and the proximity of staff and peers. Questions to ask include: is there a problem in the relationship between the student and a particular staff person or peer, does the individual prefer certain staff and peers, is the problem the result of deficits in social skills, is the size and composition of the group a factor, and does the type of interaction affect behavior? For example, an individual who prefers to be alone may tantrum when forced to join a group.

Question 3: Is the Problem Related to the Physical Environment? When the behavior occurs, note the crowdedness, noise level, temperature, lighting, level of activity, and novelty of materials. Examples of questions to ask include: is the person over or under stimulated, is there a preference for certain environmental arrangements, are novel materials and events upsetting the individual? Even if it seems unreasonable to expect that a person would want certain materials, a quiet environment, or a particular arrangement of furniture, it still is important to note if the problem behavior occurs when these conditions are not allowed or not met. For example, Greg became upset and yelled, jumped, and flailed his arms if drawers and closet doors were left open in his classroom.

Question 4: Is the Curriculum or Instructional Methods a Factor? Note the task being learned, materials, cues to respond, correction procedures, pacing, duration of task, input and response modalities, and form of the response (e.g., motor, verbal). Is the behavior related to task difficulty (e.g., motor response required of a student with poor motor skills), boredom, learning style preference (e.g., active versus passive, visual versus auditory), length of the lesson, or the manner in which the lesson is taught? For example, one young child knocked instructional materials off of the table each time a specific lesson began and ran and got other materials. She was bored with the materials that the teacher presented. Another youngster put his head down or looked away shortly after presented with a task on which he typically performed poorly.

Question 5: Is Behavior the Result of More Distant Events? Even though behavior may occur in particular contexts (e.g., school), it may, as is often true with nondisabled persons, be related to an event outside of that context. For example, the individual's home life may have been disrupted by a change in household responsibilities or the departure of a household member, or the individual may be abused. The quality of the person's life-style also might be a factor. The lives of persons with moderate or severe disabilities are often out of their control. They have few opportunities to choose their social partners, work, and living situations; the daily activities in which they engage; or the goods that they own. They often have no valued social role, or receive affection and approval only for correct performance of a task (Meyer & Evans, 1989). It is important to remedy this situation whether or not a behavior problem exists. But it is also true that such a life-style may contribute to behavior problems.

Question 6: Are There Other Person-Related Factors? Deficits in social, academic, and adaptive behavior were considered under the curriculum and instructional methods question. Other factors, whose relevance is not often acknowledged in the case of persons with moderate or severe disabilities, include those from Maslow's (1968) hierarchy: physiological needs, safety and security, belongingness and affection, self-respect, and self-actualization.

Generation of Hypotheses

Concurrent with the examination of the various aspects of the individual and his or her life is the generation of hypotheses about the behavior. Hypotheses are generated by answering two questions: Why does the individual engage in the problem behavior? and, What motivates the individual to respond (i.e., what is it about the situation that causes the individual to engage in the problem behavior)? Some reasons why individuals engage in problem behaviors and some examples of what motivates their behavior include (Donnellan et al., 1984; Evans & Meyer, 1985):

1. Emotional response. The individual's behavior may be an emotional response to fear, anger, frustration, pain, or excitement. For example, aggression might erupt due to frustration with a difficult task or boredom with a repetitive job. Self-injury may be the manifestation of fear that is caused by a change in routine. Anger might be expressed when a desired object is removed. Excitement might be the response to a favorite person's entry into the room. Professionals sometimes express the concern that "even if the individual is angry (or afraid, frustrated, and so on), he or she shouldn't express it this way; he or she must be stopped." At this stage in the process, however, it is important only to generate hypotheses about why the behavior occurs, rather than impose one's values on the individual or make statements about what should be done about the behavior.

2. Self-regulation. The individual might engage in the problem behavior (e.g., self-injury, repetitive vocal or motor behavior) in order to increase the level of arousal because the environment is unstimulating or a classroom routine is boring. Conversely, the behavior (e.g., repetitive vocal or motor behavior) might be an attempt to "block out" an environment that is overstimulating or stressful, such as too noisy or active.

3. Obtain sensory reinforcement. Behaviors (e.g., repetitive, self-injury, unusual oral behavior) may be engaged in because the input provided is reinforcing, and equivalent sensory input is unavailable elsewhere in the environment.

4. Obtain social or tangible reinforcement. The purpose of the behavior may be to elicit attention or to obtain a desired

object because of insufficient access to these reinforcers within the daily routine.

5. Self-entertainment or play. The behavior (e.g., playing with vomitus, flailing hands, hitting others) may be engaged in because the individual knows no other way to play when alone or with others.

6. Protest or avoid a situation. The purpose of the behavior may be to escape or to avoid a task or person. It may be that the task is difficult or boring, and that difficult demands are being imposed on the person.

Hypotheses Testing

If a medical basis for the problem behavior is suspected, then the parents or health professionals should be consulted. If not, the next step is to test hypotheses about the purpose and cause of the behavior. To test hypotheses, a causal factor is manipulated, and a change in behavior is noted. For example, if one hypothesis is that the student throws educational materials because he or she finds the activity boring, then the activity could be changed and the behavior monitored. If the behavior decreases, then indeed the activity was the problem. If the behavior continues with the different activity, then the activity was not the problem. If a second hypothesis is that the materials are thrown because he or she can only work for 2-minute periods, then the behavior could be monitored under brief (e.g., 1 minute) and lengthier (e.g., 4 minutes) sessions. When testing hypotheses, only one element (e.g., length of the session, the task, materials) should be changed at a time. Also, because behavior varies from day-to-day, it is necessay to test the hypotheses on several occasions.

Treatment

During the treatment step, the results of hypotheses testing are used to plan an intervention. Various approaches to intervention include:

1. The cause of the behavior is altered. If, upon analysis of the behavior, self-injury was found to be related to difficulty with an activity, then the activity could be made easier by breaking it into smaller steps, providing more assistance, or making it less aversive by providing more frequent reinforcement. Also, the functionality of the activity should be examined. If it is not functional for the student, then it should not be taught. If running away from home can be related to lack of involvement in decision making at home, then being offered a choice of activities, schedule, meals, and jobs should be provided. If avoidance is the result of a routine at home being disrupted, then a solution would be to restore the original routine.

    If the purpose of the problem behavior (e.g., stereotyped, self-abuse, rumination) is to generate sensory input (e.g., visual, auditory, tactile, olfactory, gustatory, kinesthetic) because it is otherwise unavailable in the environment, then provide an appropriate event that stimulates the same sense. For example, looking through a viewfinder or kaleidoscope could be an equivalent and more appropriate source of sensory input than flicking fingers between one's eyes and a light source. Listening to tape recorded stimuli could be an equivalent replacement for spinning objects on a hard surface.

2. Help the individual adapt to the situation. If a student throws materials because the work session is too long, then the length of the session could be shortened, then systematically increased in small increments. If a task is repetitive and causing the individual to become aggressive in response to boredom, then more frequent reinforcement might be used, then gradually reduced. If crowded conditions elicit self-injury, then the degree of crowdedness could be decreased, then slowly increased.

3. Allow the behavior to continue, but change the living, work, school, or community systems so that they support the persons and his or her behaviors. For example, educate nondisabled classmates about the purpose of the behavior,

and how to assist the student when the behavior occurs (e.g., take the child displaying the inappropriate behavior to a quiet place to relax); for employment, place the individual in a work setting that will not be disrupted by his or her inappropriate behavior or that minimizes the occurrence because it is matched to the student's preferences for the type of work, location, and so forth.

4. Teach a missing skill. If aggression is the only means a child has for initiating an interaction, then teach him or her alternative ways to initiate interactions, such as by approaching another child and offering a toy, or by gently touching a playmate. If difficulty in ascending the stairs of a public bus is causing frustration and head banging, then provide instruction to make stair climbing easier, such as use of the handrail and proper foot placement.

5. Teach the person how to communicate. Communication training is another form of teaching a missing skill. As an example of this powerful approach to altering problem behavior and enhancing communication, suppose that the purpose of a student's prolonged screaming is to escape a difficult task. The communication training approach would advocate teaching a vocalization, gesture, or other response that permits the individual to leave the task, or causes the task to be terminated. If the purpose of tantrumming is to gain a teacher's attention, then teach a gesture, sign, vocalization, or use some initial behavior of the tantrum (i.e., before the tantrum becomes intense) as a means for eliciting attention.

An important caveat here is that decreasing the problem behavior should not be the primary focus of communication instruction. The behavior problem is a manifestation of an inadequate communication system. The focus, therefore, should be on the person's overall needs and programming related to social-communicative development. Communication instruction related to behavior problems must be integrated into the larger agenda for communicative development.

COMMUNICATION TRAINING AND BEHAVIOR PROBLEMS

Model of Communication Development

The communication model is rooted in the study of the uses of language (i.e., pragmatics), and is based upon Wetherby's and Prizant's (1989) work on communicative intent and functions. Communicative intent relates to whether the individual who sends the communication signal intends for the message to affect the recipient of the message in a specific way (e.g., "I'll throw the book and maybe she won't make me do the assignment"); communicative function relates to what the goal is (e.g., to protest). Wetherby's and Prizant's (1989) description of the development of intentional communication is based upon normal child development. It progresses along two dimensions: the vertical development of intentionality dimension, and the horizontal development of intentionality or communicative function dimension. In assessing problem behavior from a communication standpoint, it is important to consider both dimensions. The results have direct implications for the level of complexity of the communication system.

Vertical Dimension of Intentionality The vertical dimension of intentionality describes how intentionality emerges. Wetherby and Prizant (1989) describe six levels of intentionality in the vertical dimension, as adapted from the work of Harding (1984) and Sugarman (1984). These are described below, along with a problem behavior (i.e., screaming), to illustrate how an individual at each level might use the behavior. It is assumed that an analysis of behavior indicated that the young female student who displays the screaming behavior does so when she is taken outdoors from the classroom. It is important to recognize, however, that one cannot assess intentionality on the basis of a single behavior. Wetherby's and Prizant's (1989) six levels of intentionality and an example at each level are as follows:

1. There is no awareness of a goal. For example, the individual demonstrates "a diffuse fuss or reaction to a nonspecific situation to express an emotion such as frustration, anger, excitement, and pleasure" (Wetherby & Prizant, 1989, p. 79). As for the student who screams, he or she would do so when he or she became aware that he or she was outdoors, and not sooner, such as while being accompanied to the door.

2. The individual is aware of a goal that might be shown by focusing attention on or vocalizing toward a person or an object. The student who screams would do so upon reaching the door to go outside, and he or she would focus attention on the door or what lies beyond, making it obvious that the screams are in response to going outdoors.

3. There is a simple plan to achieve a goal. Actions may be directed toward a person. In the example, the child would direct the screams to the person accompanying her, indicating that she knows the person could decide whether or not to take her outdoors. However, she would not combine other actions such as looking from the person to the door.

4. There is a coordinated plan to achieve a goal. Here, the youngster, while continuing to scream, would alternate looking at the door and to the person accompanying her, or to another indoor location. She might also combine screaming at the person, and waiting for a response. At this level, the person can coordinate multiple signals to communicate a message more clearly. Another example would be an individual who leads an adult to a shelf where there is a desired object that is out of reach.

5. There are alternative plans used to achieve a goal. At this point, if the goal of not going outdoors was not achieved by screaming, the child would try an alternative behavior, such as hitting her head or running away.

6. The plan to achieve a goal is developed after the individual reflects upon past outcomes, and the projected success or failure of various alternatives (i.e., pragmatic awareness). The child who screams would be able to devise alternative

approaches by thinking them through without needing to directly try them.

It is important to recognize that the six levels in the vertical dimension represent a continuum of intentionality, from the most basic to more complex forms. There is no single point in the continuum at which a person is suddenly intentional. Furthermore, intentionality cannot be viewed in isolation. As is evident in the above descriptions, intentionality is linked to cognitive, motor, and social development. For example, in order for more complex forms of intentionality to be displayed, the individual must understand the separateness of the self from the environment, begin to interact with others, become aware of objects and their uses, and understand causality and means/ends. This is not to say that these are necessary prerequisites to the development of intentionality. They may, in fact, emerge concurrently with and be intertwined with its development. It is also not implied that communication instruction should be delayed until the individual demonstrates complex forms of intentionality, such as having a simple plan to achieve a goal.

For example, if a person is aware of goals, but demonstates no simple plans to achieve them, a partner would attempt to promote intentional communicative behavior by responding as if the individual was capable of planning to achieve his or her goals. Using the example of the screaming child, if she was aware of a goal, but had no simple plan to achieve it, her attention to a partner could be prompted, and then her screaming responded to by taking her to a preferred indoor location. More complex and indirect forms of interaction might also be successful, such as shifting her gaze between a person and a preferred indoor location or using an object that she is assisted to look at or touch to denote an alternative location. However, the results may not occur as quickly when using the more complex forms in comparison to the more direct communication method that was described first.

Horizontal Dimension: Communicative Function or Goal

The horizontal dimension is comprised of the various functions (i.e., goals) that communicative behavior can fulfill (see Table

2.1). These functions can be used to determine the breadth of an individual's communicative behavior (i.e., does it serve a single function such as requesting an action, or many different ones). In distinguishing between communicative intent and function, Wetherby and Prizant (1989) indicate that communicative intent requires that the sender of the signal have a goal (e.g., "I want to avoid going outside"), and that there be an awareness of the possible effect of the signal on the communication partner (e.g., "If I scream, they might let me stay inside"). Communicative function means that the signal produced an outcome (e.g., the teacher told her to quit screaming, the teacher let her remain indoors). Effective communication involves sending a message that produces the result that the sender intended. However, behavior can also serve a function or have a function assigned, even when there is no underlying intent to a person's actions (Wetherby & Prizant, 1989). In fact, this may be the case in many instances in which communication instruction is used with problem behaviors. A function can be assigned to a behavior. For example, protesting might be assigned to a student's tantrums.

Communicative functions can be used as a guide when designing or expanding an individual's communication system. These communicative functions are described in more detail in Table 2.1 and in Chapter Three (pp. 41–48).

Issues Related to Communicative Intent and Function
There are several issues to keep in mind when assessing communicative intent and function and in developing communication programs. First, assessment of intent is often difficult because it may need to be inferred from observable behavior, such as the individual's persistence in using a behavior, the cessation of a behavior when the goal is met, and emotions or other indicators of satisfaction or dissatisfaction when a goal is, or is not, met (Wetherby & Prizant, 1989). Assessment becomes even more difficult in the case of individuals who have motor problems or limited behavioral repertoires. For example, it can be difficult to clearly ascertain that a youngster is shifting his or her gaze between a communication partner and an object if head control is poor and he or she has many other

Table 2.1. Horizontal development of intentional communication in the emerging language of normal children

A. Behavioral regulation
1. Request object—acts used to demand a desired tangible object
2. Request action—acts used to command another to carry out an action
3. Protest—acts used to refuse an undesired object or to command another to cease an undesired action

B. Social interaction
1. Request social routine—acts used to command another to commence or continue carrying out a game-like social interaction
2. Greet—acts used to gain another's attention, to indicate notice of their presence, or to indicate notice of the initiation or termination of an interaction
3. Show off—acts used to attract another's attention to oneself
4. Call—acts used to gain the attention of others, usually to indicate that a communicative act is to follow
+5. Request permission—acts used to seek another's consent to carry out an action; involves the child carrying out or wishing to carry out the action
+6. Acknowledgment—acts used to indicate notice of another person's previous statement or action

C. Joint attention
1. Comment on object—acts used to direct another's attention to an entity
2. Comment on action—acts used to direct another's attention to an event
+3. Clarification—acts used to clarify the previous utterance
+4. Request information—acts used to seek information, explanations, or clarifications about an object, event, or previous utterance; includes wh-questions and other utterances having the intonation contour of an interrogative

From Wetherby, A. M., & Prizant, B. M. (1989). The expression of communicative intent: Assessment guidelines. *Seminars in Speech and Language, 10* (1), 80; reprinted by permission of Thieme Medical Publishers, Inc., and from Wetherby, A., Cain, D., Yonclas, D., & Walker, V. (1988). Analysis of intentional communication of normal children from the prelinguistic to the multi-word stage. *Journal of Speech and Hearing Research, 31,* p. 244.

+May not emerge until the one-word or multiword stage.

random head and eye movements. Another example would be a student whose motor impairments prevent him or her from showing satisfaction or dissatisfaction through body movements or emotions. In cases such as these, it may be necessary to work with therapists to find optimal positions for enhancing motor movement. It may also be necessary to observe the individual for subtle behaviors such as changes in muscle tone, changes in levels of alertness, and withdrawal. Finally, the individual may need to be given more time to respond.

Second, an individual's intentional behavior may appear limited, when, in fact, it was extinguished because it was not attended to in the past. By responding to the individual's existing behaviors, this problem should be overcome. Another approach would be to set up communicative temptations to which the individual must respond in order to achieve a desired outcome. This is discussed in Wetherby and Prizant (1989) and later in this chapter. Third, the environment may inhibit the individual's display of intentional behavior. For example, he or she may be provided with so much assistance in daily routines that it is unnecessary for the individual to communicate. The obvious solution would be to delay assistance and to wait for a response.

Fourth, communication instruction may be inappropriate in cases of self-injury or severe aggression, when a quicker means for changing the behavior is available, such as eliminating an event that elicits the behavior. Fifth, when past efforts to teach communication skills have failed, therapists sometimes indicate that the prognosis for further development is poor. However, there are individuals with whom extensive therapy has been unsuccessful, yet who have developed communication skills that serve the same function as a problem behavior. Evidently, the situations surrounding problem behaviors are meaningful and highly motivating for the individual. It is not unusual for this instruction to serve as a springboard for broader communication development.

Sixth, it is not unusual for individuals to utilize more than one method to communicate. For whatever reasons, even persons who have some communication will sometimes engage in problem behaviors (e.g., a verbally competent 5-year-old throwing a tantrum). It may be that their communication systems are inadequate, that more appropriate communication efforts were ineffective, or that displaying problem behavior is a more efficient means.

Assessment

There are numerous methods for obtaining information about the communicative intents or functions of problem behavior. Four methods will be described in this section. *The Motivation Assessment Scale* (MAS) (Durand & Crimmins, 1988) is a 16-item questionnaire that is completed by persons well acquainted with the individual with a disability. It is useful in assessing the communicative function of problem behavior. Examples of items include: "Would this behavior occur continuously if your child was left alone for long periods of time? (e.g., 1 hour)," and "Does this behavior occur when any request is made of your child?" After scoring each item on a scale of zero to six, where zero represents "Never" and six represents "Always," the scores on specific item clusters are totaled. Higher scores are predictive of the purposes served by the problem behavior. The MAS items correspond to four common motivational factors for problem behavior—to obtain a tangible reinforcer, to gain attention, to escape, or to self-stimulate.

The *Communication Interview* (see Appendix A.1; Schuler, Peck, Willard, & Theimer, 1989) also is completed by someone who is well acquainted with the individual. This form (Figure 2.1) was designed to gather information about communicative means (e.g., tantrum), functions (e.g., protest), and the contexts in which behaviors occur (e.g., when an adult terminates an interaction). This form lists some of the primary categories of communicative function (e.g., requests for affection/ interaction, protest, declaration/comment), along with sample contexts in each category (e.g., the "protest" category includes: "common routine is dropped," "favorite toy/food taken away"). Listed along the top of the form are various means of communication, which include problem behaviors (e.g., crying, aggression, tantrum/self-injury) and appropriate responses (e.g., nods "yes," one-word speech). To complete the form, the interviewee indicates, for each communicative function item, the behavior(s) that is often used to express it. Comments can be added, such as to indicate, when multiple behaviors are used for the same function, the order in which they occur or if a behavior serves different functions in different situations (e.g., school versus home). Completion of the interview provides information about which behaviors (i.e., means) are used and for which functions (i.e., ends). It can also identify a behavior that serves multiple functions, or behaviors that are combined to serve a function. Intentionality can be inferred from "the diversification of those means and functions and the concurrent use of multiple means and functions" (Schuler & Prizant, 1987).

A third method, which can be used to assess both intentionality and function, is to arrange situations that entice the individual to communicate (Schuler et al., 1989; Wetherby & Prizant, 1989). While this method was not developed specifically for problem behaviors, it is still applicable. Examples of how situations can be arranged include: 1) engage the individual in a commonly executed routine (e.g., washing hands) and place a needed object (e.g., soap) out of sight or out of reach; 2) on the way to a favorite activity in another room, do not open the door so that the student can progress to the activity; 3) place a favorite item in a clear, plastic bottle, and place it within reach with the lid tightly fastened (Schuler et al., 1989; Wetherby & Prizant, 1989); and 4) engage the individual in a favorite activity for a few trials, then do the activity with another person (Wetherby & Prizant, 1989). If a student does not respond to the initial communicative temptation, Schuler et al. (1989) recommend that the temptation be varied. For example, a variation of placing a desired item (e.g., tape recorder) out of reach, is to allow the student to briefly use it before it is placed out of reach.

During the arranged events, note the means the student uses to communicate (e.g., vocalizations, looking, pointing). Also, consider intentionality. Is the individual aware of a goal? Does he or she interact directly with objects and persons, or

Communication Interview

Cue Questions:	Crying	Aggression	Tantrums/Self-injury	Passive Gaze	Proximity	Pulling other's hands	Touching/moving other's face	Grabs/reaches	Enactment	Removes self/walks away	Vocalization/noise	Active gaze	Gives object	Gestures/pointing	Facial expression	Shakes "no"/nods "yes"	Intonation	Inappropriate echolalia	Appropriate echolalia	One-word speech	One-word signs	Complex speech	Complex signs
1. Requests for affection/interaction: WHAT IF S WANTS																							
Adult to sit near?																							
Peer to sit near?																							
Nonhandicapped peer to sit near?																							
Adult to look at him or her?																							
Adult to tickle him or her?																							
To cuddle or embrace?																							
To sit on adult's lap?																							
Other:																							
2. Requests for adult action: WHAT IF S WANTS																							
Help with dressing?																							
To be read a book?																							

To play ball/a game?

To go outside/to store?

Other:

3. Requests for object, food, or things: WHAT IF S WANTS

An object out of reach?

A door/container opened?

A favorite food?

Music/radio/television?

Keys/toy/book?

Other:

4. Protest: WHAT IF

Common routine is dropped?

Favorite toy/food taken away?

Taken for ride without desire?

Adult terminates interaction?

Required to do something he or she doesn't want to do?

Other:

5. Declaration/comment: WHAT IF S WANTS

To show you something?

You to look at something?

Other:

Figure 2.1. Example of a communication interview checklist. (From Schuler, A.L., Peck, C.A., Willard, C., & Theimer, K. [1989]. Assessment of communicative means and functions through interview: Assessing the communicative capabilities of individuals with limited language. *Seminars in Speech and Language, 10(1),* 54; reprinted by permission of Thieme Medical Publishers, Inc.)

indirectly, such as by eliciting assistance? If assistance is not forthcoming, does the individual repair the strategy by using another means?

A fourth strategy is to prepare an anecdotal record (see Appendix A.2 for a blank form; Alberto & Troutman, 1986). This involves observing or videotaping the student in various contexts (e.g., home, school, community, with a group, alone) and recording a description of the problem behavior, the time it occurs, the linguistic and nonlinguistic events that precede and follow the behavioral occurrence, and any accompanying behaviors. A sample anecdotal record is shown in Figure 2.2. Analysis of the anecdotal record seeks to identify consistent relationships between antecedents and the problem behavior. The relationship can include linguistic antecedents, such as a request for an action (e.g., "stand up") or a greeting, and non-linguistic events, such as an increase in noise level, placing program materials on the desk, or a change in instructor or peer group. The anecdotal record should also be analyzed for consistent relationships between behavior and its consequences. For example, when a student tantrums, does the teacher frequently end the task, turn away, or provide attention? In behavioral terms, these may be reinforcing consequences that strengthen or maintain behavior. From a communication standpoint, these consequences may mean that the behavior is achieving its intended goal (i.e., is serving a communicative function).

Hypotheses Testing

In some cases, there will be uncertainty about the accuracy of the hypotheses regarding the cause and function of problem behavior. Evans and Meyer (1985) suggest testing the explanations prior to generating interventions. For example, if it is hypothesized that a student bites his or her arm in order to escape a difficult task, the hypothesis could be tested by making the task easier, such as by breaking it down into smaller steps. This should result in a decrease in tantrums when this task is presented. Another example, if tantrums are believed to

Anecdotal Recording

Student: Sara   Teacher: Ben   Observer: Tammy

Date: 5/15/90   Begin time: 8:30 A.M.   End time: 3:00 P.M.

Locations: Classroom, school grounds, bus, store

Behavior: Biting self: bringing teeth into contact with arm or hand; hitting others: swinging arm and making contact with hand/fist.

Time	Antecedent	Behavior	Consequence
8:30	On school bus, a peer asked her to stand.	Bit herself and hit the peer on the arm.	Peer said, "Come," assisted her to stand and walk from bus.
8:35	Standing in the classroom with three other students nearby, Ben asked her to, "Go hang coat."	Bit herself and hit Tom (peer).	Ben stopped her from hitting again and held her hand as they walked to the coat rack.
9:00	Ben puts away instructional materials used for practicing paying for purchases. Todd (another student) gets up and goes to coat rack. Next activity is going shopping in the community.	Bit herself, then vocalized, "Mum, mum, mum" and slapped Marsha (peer) on face.	Ben yelled, "Sara," and ran to Marsha to interrupt the slapping.
		Sara bit herself again.	Ben turned her and prompted her to walk to the coat rack.
10:00	At the cashier after paying for groceries at Main Street Grocery, with Ben, he told her, "Time to go."	Bumped into Ben while she bit her hand.	Ben said, "It's o.k., Sara. Let's go outside," and assisted her to walk from the store.

Figure 2.2. Sample anecdotal recording.

be associated with the inaccessibility of a desired object that is in view, then the amount of tantrums should decrease if the object is kept out of view or made fully accessible. More rigorous testing would involve single subject experimental designs. The reader is referred to sources that explain these procedures (Tawney & Gast, 1984), and to examples of their application related to testing hypotheses about problem behavior (Carr & Durand, 1985; Durand & Carr, 1987). However, a caveat is that hypotheses testing may be unethical in cases in which the problem behavior must be immediately addressed because it threatens the health or safety of the individual or others in the environment.

SUMMARY

This chapter, with an underlying assumption that problem behavior is a form of communication often overlooked in persons with severe disabilities, outlines questions to ask and strategies to employ when exploring and/or confirming various possible messages. A number of available tools to use in this process are discussed along with the schema of Wetherby and Prizant (1989) as a guide to a range of possible intents and messages. The next chapter on "getting started" utilizes this approach to guide efforts to identify forms and functions of behaviors as they occur throughout a typical daily schedule.

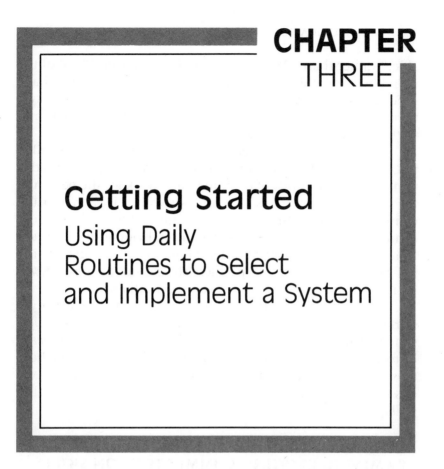

CHAPTER THREE

Getting Started
Using Daily
Routines to Select
and Implement a System

Children, adolescents, and adults talk about what is familiar to them. Their knowledge comes from personal experiences in daily interactions with the world of people, objects, and events. The ability to express this knowledge is developed through shared attention and activity with significant communication partners (Bruner, 1974/1975). This bidirectional nature of communication has direct implications for getting started with augmentative communication. An augmentative system is not just words laid out in dictionary fashion, it is a system for communicating.

When augmenting an individual's communicative effectiveness is discussed, professionals often are lured by catalogue pictures of materials and equipment. Decisions about the format of a communication system are in terms of, "What's available," rather than, "What are the individual needs." All of the individuals mentioned in the case histories that follow have unique competencies in the area of communication. The systems designed for them reflect those competencies first, and "What's available," second.

The philosophies shared by the authors have been detailed in Chapter One. An overriding assumption in getting started is that the words or units of meaning must work for the person in the individual's existing social contexts with at least their usual communication partners. That is, the units chosen to represent certain meanings must empower the individual to become a legitimate communicator in their familiar surroundings. Existing signals, activities, and partners should not be ignored. All individuals have some form of communication.

The purpose of this chapter is to help the reader to get started with an augmentative or alternative communication system that has a high likelihood of being successful. The case histories in the following sections provide examples of how these principles were applied by different professionals in various settings. The first target in all cases was to examine existing skills.

EXAMINING EXISTING COMMUNICATION SKILLS

Rationale

All behavior communicates (McDonald, 1985). Sometimes the individual intentionally communicates an idea and sometimes the partner interprets the message "as if" the individual was trying to convey a particular thought. Some behaviors are more conventional, or more widely understood, than others. For example, if a child looks at a spinning top, then looks at the adult and smiles when the top stops, the adult will likely respond as if the child had said, "More." This gaze pattern is understood by more people than, for instance, brief calming when the top stops.

There is no question that individuals with moderate to

severe disabilities should be encouraged to use the most conventional and socially appropriate signals possible when communicating. However, the mutuality of interaction must first be established: the person must understand that he or she can be or is an active and acceptable participant in communicative exchanges. If the individual is not already aware of this power through communicating, he or she can be assisted to realize the effect of the signals by establishing, maintaining, and terminating joint attention and activity. If the individual is aware of this power, he or she can be assisted to become even more efficient in manipulating his or her environment by using new, more conventional and acceptable signals. Three steps are provided below to help in examining existing communication signals.

Step One—Examine Existing Signals in Typical Schedules A first step is to examine current signals in terms of their content, form, function, and context. The content of the signal refers to its meaning. Some individuals have many meanings to express—they have sorted various types of environmental information into categories and have developed a sense of how the categories are interrelated. For example, John points to a picture of a "dog" whenever he sees medium to small, four-legged animal (e.g., cat, goat, sheep), whereas he points to a picture of a "horse" whenever he sees large, four-legged animals (e.g., elephants, cows, deer). Contradictorily, Jane uses the picture of a "dog" to refer to her own dog and no others. The content of John's "dog" is much more flexible than that of Jane's.

The form of a signal refers to two aspects of communication: the behavior exhibited by the individual and the symbol system used with the behavior. For example, Sue points to an empty cup to indicate a request for a drink. The behavior exhibited is pointing. The symbol system is the use of an empty cup to refer to a cup with drink in it. Joe uses the sign, "DRINK," to request liquids. The behavior involves a manual movement, and the symbolic system is sign language. In the former case, the behavior and the symbol are quite separate. In the latter case, the behavior is assumed according to the requirements for the use of the symbolic system of signing. Other behaviors include gaze, pointing, vocalization, arm tensing, hand movements, or calming in the presence of a stimulus. Symbolic systems include pictures, objects, spoken words, written words, and sign language.

The intent or function of the signal might be thought of as the job the signal performs. Wetherby and Prizant (1989) have provided a list of communicative intents that relates to prelinguistic and linguistic communication signals. This list was provided in Chapter Two. Prelinguistic signals are the communication forms used by an individual prior to the development of a conventional linguistic system, such as spoken English. Many of the individuals discussed in the case histories are prelinguistic communicators. According to Wetherby and Prizant (1989), children who develop language normally, as well as those who have difficulty, use their communication signals to perform a variety of functions. Generally, prelinguistic and early linguistic signals have three effects: 1) regulating the behavior of others, 2) establishing and maintaining social interaction, and 3) establishing or maintaining more specific attention to objects and events. Specific functions such as protesting, requesting, or greeting can be thought of as fulfilling one of these three more general functions.

The context of the signal includes the settings, partners, and daily routines and activities that constitute the individual's typical interaction environments. Signals may vary according to where the individual is communicating (e.g., at home versus in a restaurant), with whom the individual is interacting (e.g., parent versus classroom aide), and the familiarity of the sequences of events within daily experiences (e.g., toileting versus going bowling for the first time).

In some of the case histories that follow, the practitioners have started the process by having all significant communication partners complete a daily schedule of the individual's typical routines. An example of a composite schedule is provided in Table 3.1. As can be seen, Sean has several activities that are common across settings including greetings, dressing, meals, toileting, grooming, and playtimes. These activities can be examined to determine if, and in what form, communication

Table 3.1. Example of Sean's combined weekday schedule

Time	Home: Parents	School: Teacher	Daycare: Teacher
7:30	Get up, grooming, dressing		
8:00	Breakfast		
8:20	Grooming, coat on		
8:30	To school bus		
8:45		Greeting, coat off	
9:00		Morning Circle	
9:25		Work stations— Fine motor, concept matching	
9:55		Playtime— Chooses activity	
10:10		Coats on, line up	
10:15		Recess	
10:30		Coats off, toileting, wash hands and face	
10:40		Snack	
11:00		Therapy— Occupational and physical	
11:30		Coats on, to bus	
11:50			Greeting, coat off
12:00		Lunch	
12:30			Playtime
1:30			Sesame Street
2:30			Playtime
3:00			Snack
3:30			Playtime
5:00	Greeting, drive home		Coat on
5:30	Coat off, play, wash hands		
6:00	Dinner		
6:30	Television or play		
8:30	Wash, brush teeth, pajamas on, look at book		

already occurs or could be encouraged. In addition, these activities can be examined to determine possible needs for expression from Sean's perspective.

To determine the existing forms of communication, each partner provides a verbal or written description of the sequence of actions and typical communication signals given by the partner and/or the individual with disabilities within any one specific common activity, such as grooming. This process can be thought of as "retrospective" rather than direct observation. In essence, partners are asked to summarize their observations of the signals they remember typically being used during these activities, what the signals meant, and how they were responded to by the partner. In most cases, the authors have found retrospective observation to be a valid measure of communication skills and an excellent technique to use to target where more specific information may be needed.

For example, Sean's father related a usual sequence of grooming (e.g., washing face, brushing hair, and brushing teeth) at home. When asked to describe communication signals during this activity, the father remembered that Sean always wanted to brush his teeth first. The signal Sean used was to grab his toothbrush when he went into the bathroom. The father noted, however, that he always made Sean put the toothbrush down until his face had been washed and hair brushed.

Sean's teacher was asked to provide more detail about the 10:30 activity. The sequence in this setting was toileting, washing hands, and brushing hair. After toileting, Sean usually opened the cupboard and took out his brush. The teacher preferred that Sean wash his hands before brushing his hair so that the brush handle stayed clean.

In the case of Sean, a wealth of information was gleaned through this process:

1. The content and elements of the grooming activity at home and at school were similar with the exception of toothbrush and toothpaste. Sean was familiar with soap, faucets, towels, and hairbrushes. He was also familiar with

several bathroom settings that have common elements such as a sink and toilet.

2. The form of Sean's signal is to reach out and take the item he wants. The form is recognized by his father and his teacher.

3. The signal was probably intended to be a request to use that object; however, in both settings, the request was denied.

4. The sequence at home, although established, was arbitrarily ordered according to the parent's preference and, very likely, the need to finish grooming in a reasonable timeframe. The sequence for grooming at school was established to follow what the teacher felt to be a more hygienic order.

Step Two—Collect Information from Other Sources After collecting and reviewing information from retrospective and anecdotal sources, direct observations of the individual with different partners in various settings are conducted. This enables the observer to confirm the evidence of particular communication signals that was noted through retrospective observation and to determine the effect of specific communication situations on the form and function of the signal. In the case histories, several examples of observation forms were used (contained in the Appendix).

Additionally, planned activities can be used to elicit particular behaviors. These activities may include the specific types of testing that are discussed in Chapter Two. They may also consist of nondirective "communication temptations" (cf. Wetherby & Prizant, 1989) such as putting desired items in sight but out of reach and then looking at the individual and the item expectantly. The latter techniques lead to responses from the individual that can be analyzed for content, form, and function in an integrated manner. For example, if an individual shows a preference for having a hair dryer blow warm air on his or her arm, the adult can unexpectedly turn the hair dryer off, saying, "All done," and then look at the individual expectantly. The individual might touch the hair dryer and look at the adult. If the adult remains quiet or says, "What?," the individual might persist by pushing the hair dryer toward the adult. The content of the signal indicates a knowledge of the relationship between warm air, the hair dryer, and the adult who can activate it. The behavioral form of the signal includes touching plus looking at the adult. The symbolic form of the signal is to use the actual object, the hair dryer, to represent itself. The function of the signal is to request "more."

Step Three—Answer Specific Questions Use the combined data regarding the individual's content, forms, functions, and contexts to answer the following questions:

1. What behavioral forms or signals does the individual use in various settings? Remembering that all behavior communicates, self-injurious behavior, "self-stimulatory" behavior, subtle movements of facial features, or whole limb/body movements need to be considered as well as the more obvious communicative behaviors of gaze, gesture, and vocalization. Schuler et al.'s (1989) "Communication Interview" form, discussed in Chapter Two and displayed in Appendix A.1, addressed commonly seen behaviors and their functions.

2. What symbolic forms are recognized by the individual? A formal matching task could be used to assess knowledge of the relationship between pictures and objects. Information from observations may reveal that the individual uses play objects as if they were real, recognizes pictures as being representative of real objects, or needs the actual object to respond appropriately. The initial communication system should either use familiar symbolic forms to maximize the chance for success or focus on teaching a limited set of behaviors to relate to one or two socially-appropriate symbolic forms.

3. Is the individual aware that his or her signal has a particular effect on the partner? A continuum of intentionality, discussed in Chapter Two and developed by Wetherby and Prizant (1989), could be used as a guide in this difficult

process. Briefly, intentionality is seen as an emerging behavior that begins with early reflexive actions performed with no obvious awareness that the behavior of others will be affected. It continues to develop as the child becomes aware that some effect was achieved as the result of his or her actions and then the child begins to plan ahead, in an increasingly complex manner, ways in which to affect others. The determination of degree of intentionality affects the complexity of an augmentative system. An individual who is not clearly manipulating others to achieve goals will need repeated experiences with the consequences of his or her signal prior to using a more complex form for this purpose.

4. How many functions or jobs does this behavioral form accomplish? Does a gaze serve only to request food or does it also signal a request for the continuation of a social ritual such as greeting? It is quite typical for one signal to serve many functions. Do all partners respond to the signal in the same way? It may be discovered that one partner thinks the signal is a request for an item while the other thinks it is a comment about the item. Agreement as to the function of a behavioral form is not necessary in all cases. However, those forms with an agreed-upon function should be targeted for an initial communication system.

5. How many forms are associated with each function? Just as one signal can serve a variety of functions, one function such as requesting or greeting can be accomplished by using a variety of forms. For instance, in one case history, the function of protest or rejection is expressed by pushing away objects or people, hitting, biting, and putting the head down.

6. How stable or consistent is the form in appearance? Often, the signals of individuals with moderate or severe disabilities differ slightly in their topography each time they are used. For example, gaze may be steady one time and brief the next. An individual may touch and look at novel items, but only touch familiar items without giving them

visual attention. Instability in the form of the signal may be one reason why partners are unable to respond consistently.

7. When there is variation in the signal, what effect does this have on the partner's response? Do partners ignore these differences and allow the signal to function in the same way? Or, does the variation lead to confusion and inconsistency of response from the partner?

8. Who is responding to the signals and in what context? Perhaps only the classroom aide is able to interpret the individual in more than one situation. Or perhaps the parents report a particular signal at home that has not been seen at school. To be maximally effective, the signal should be recognized in many settings with many partners. The team may need to instruct partners to respond to the behavioral forms.

9. What is the frequency with which the signal is used? How many opportunities for signaling are provided by communication partners? Low frequency of requesting, for example, may be directly related to having few opportunities for making a choice or to the partner's expectation that the individual is not competent to express his or her desires. When each partner is giving details about his or her daily schedule with the individual, the question could be, "How often does the individual have an opportunity to tell you what he or she wants?"

ESTABLISHING
CONSISTENCY WITH EXISTING SIGNALS

Once the individual's current signals have been described in terms of content, form, function, and context, it is important to make the signals more efficient. If the current signals are responded to consistently, the individual is ready to move on to more conventional signals. In many cases, however, the focus remains on either producing signals more consistently or assuring more consistent responses to signals.

Five Step Process

Generally, five steps have been used in the case studies to establish consistency with existing signals. They are summarized below.

Step One—Agree upon Partner Response and the Context Since the individual already has the signal in his or her repertoire, the focus is on establishing consistent partner responses. All regular communication partners need to agree upon a response to a particular signal. This will allow the signal to become meaningful across communicative interactions. The context in which the signal will be responded to should also be agreed upon. For example, the parents, teacher, and support staff may agree to let a gaze at an object or food serve as a request during mealtimes and playtime when an adult is near. However, gazing at an object during other activities, such as recess when an adult is not near, will not be considered a request signal. This clarifies the contextual uses of communicative signals for the individual and makes it possible for the adults to respond in a predictable manner.

Step Two—Instruct Partners to Identify the Signal If the signal is difficult to identify, the partners may not be able to respond consistently. For example, Donna, a 3-year-old with cerebral palsy and visual and hearing impairments, displayed behaviors that seemed to be unrelated to the events that were surrounding her. Additionally, Donna's teacher and classroom aide noted that it was difficult to understand her because her behavioral repertoire was limited. Each partner had a different idea of what each particular behavior meant. The teacher, the physical therapist, and the communications disorders specialist (CDS) had chosen an existing behavior (e.g., slight body tensing) as a signal for "more." However, other partners were not able to identify the movement.

To ameliorate this confusion, a rocking routine, which was already part of her tactile-kinesthetic program, was chosen as an instructional situation. Donna was held in the adult's lap while they sat in a rocking chair. As the chair was moved back and forth, the adult would say, "Rock, rock, rock, rock," in a rhythmic manner. In the midst of this movement, the adult would stop the chair, saying, "Stop," and wait for a whole body tensing movement. When Donna moved, the adult said, "More" and the rocking was continued. The teacher directly trained the other partners to accept the agreed-upon signal. Data was taken on the number of times these new partners identified Donna's signal within this routine. Videotapes were used to train her family, who lived quite a distance from school, and less-frequent communication partners.

Step Three—Create New Opportunities If the frequency of the signal is low, it may be necessary to create new opportunities within existing ones to allow the signal to be used more frequently. Adding pauses, interruptions, and delays in already established routines, such as the rocking routine with Donna, gives the individual a chance to take a turn in the familiar conversation (Halle, 1985). Providing choices in controlled activities gives the individual a chance to express personal preferences. Occasionally "misunderstanding" and providing the wrong item gives the individual a chance to repair the mistake and express his or her preference again. Models and decreasing levels of prompting allow the individual to communicate at the appropriate time in the routine using existing skills.

For example, John, an 18-year-old with cerebral palsy and moderate disabilities, had a fairly large picture vocabulary and used the word, "No!" in an extremely loud voice to protest when his frustration level was extreme. His family wanted him to use "no" in a more polite manner for protesting and for rejecting an item before his frustration reached this level.

By examining John's typical daily schedule, the family and the intervention team decided to begin by targeting grooming as a time to provide more opportunities for protesting and rejecting using the word "no." Grooming occurred several times during the day across settings and partners, and it was a routine that John enjoyed. It was decided that picture choices were to be presented for brushing hair, brushing teeth, washing hands or face, all preferred items, and for shaving cream and razor, two nonpreferred items. The choices were taped around the mirror at school.

As John finished one task during grooming, the adult would look expectantly at John and at the pictures of possible remaining tasks. John would point to his preference. The adult complied in some instances and, in others, purposely misunderstood and brought out a nonpreferred item, saying, "Razor? You want razor?," followed by a pause and expectant look at John. At first, John pushed the nonpreferred item away and pointed again to his choice. The adult modeled, "No? No razor?," using a quiet voice and then complying. After this sequence had been modeled several times within one grooming session, the adult persisted in presenting the razor even after John had gently pushed it away. John finally said "No" in a quiet voice much like the model during this first trial grooming session. He continued to use it in following sessions with fewer and fewer models. His mother observed one session at school and reported some success at home.

Once the team is familiar with the individual's schedule, a decision is made regarding which routines to pause, delay, or interrupt in order to encourage more active participation in communicative exchanges. The key factors here are familiarity and predictability. The routine must be familiar to the individual so that he or she can predict what happens next. When the partner delays his or her usual response, the individual often will fill in the missing portion of the routine. For example, when the individual is holding a toothbrush, about to brush his or her teeth, the toothpaste could be placed in sight, but out of reach. The adult could delay getting the toothpaste, as usual, until the individual signals a request for it in some way. Or, an instant coffee container could be left empty, near the hot water. During break, a staff member could wait nearby until the person commented or asked for more coffee before refilling the container.

Similarly, an examination of typical daily activities will reveal situations in which choices could be made available without disrupting the flow of activities. For example, if John were given a choice of brushing his teeth, brushing his hair, shaving, or washing during the morning grooming time, he might not be finished in order to get to high school on time. However, his mother could ask John which grooming task he wants to do first and then set the order of the remaining tasks herself. The teacher may have dedicated a longer time period for grooming as part of a self-help objective. He or she may give John the opportunity to make choices throughout the routine until it is finished. An important part of learning to make choices is recognizing that there are times when choosing is limited. Later, perhaps, John could be given more independence by his parents for this routine as he begins to express preferences more clearly.

Step Four—Expand the System to New Settings When the familiar partners are responding consistently, the team may want to expand the number of activities or settings in which the signal is accepted. For example, if the signal is recognized consistently during grooming at home and at school, perhaps it could be recognized in a public restroom at a shopping center. It is important to make the system maximally efficient in as many daily activities as possible.

Step Five—Change or Fade Levels of Instructional Assistance to Less Intrusive Levels By examining the details of routines, the team can become aware of the balance between instructionally cued responses and naturally cued initiations or responses. A cue is a stimulus that occurs before a particular behavior is performed. It is often assumed that "teaching" should involve numerous verbal cues. Researchers, such as Falvey, Brown, Lyon, Baumgart, and Schroeder (1980), Halle (1985), and McDonald (1985), challenge this assumption. Many of the cues used for communication arise from natural conditions such as hunger or needing help. When a high percentage of instructional verbal cues are used, in essence, individuals are taught to ignore the natural cues and wait for some cue from the instructor. To illustrate, a common training method is to withhold a desired item until the individual touches or points to the object. A verbal cue may be quickly provided, such as, "Point to 'juice', Sammy," without waiting to see what

Sammy will do when the juice is presented. If Sammy wants the juice and the adult holds it back looking expectantly at Sammy after he has consumed eight salty crackers, Sammy is likely to reach for the juice. When the adult cues verbally, he or she needs to be aware that Sammy's chance to initiate has been eliminated. The passivity often described in case studies of individuals with moderate to severe mental retardation may, in some cases, be a result of overuse of instructional cues.

The five steps presented above are procedures that establish consistency for the form and use of signals. The case studies provide more detailed accounts of how these steps were used in each unique circumstance. The point of this chapter is that before new systems are developed for an individual, the existing communication forms and functions must be recognized by the individual and by familiar partners as legitimate. This provides the foundation for shaping new forms of signals, recognizing new symbols, and using them to perform more varied functions of communication.

SUCCESSFUL STARTS

In closing, the authors would like to share personal observations regarding successfully implemented augmentative and alternative communication systems. When the authors reflect on those communication systems that did and did not work, common threads become evident, such as:

1. Successful communication systems often have one excited, committed person spearheading the efforts. This person is usually willing to examine his or her own communicative behaviors and to take on the responsibility of coordinating the team and even constructing the system, when necessary.
2. Successful starts have been made when the symbolic level of the system matches the individual's ability or when the expectation for what the individual will learn is adjusted. This is where the glamour of catalogues can interfere with

common sense. If an individual would rather eat pictures or tear pictures than look at them, he or she may not have the symbolic capability to understand the representation that is intended. In the case history of Kevin in Chapter Six, a signing system was attempted. Kevin showed only limited use of one or two signs, requiring prompts in most instances. Sign language is a highly symbolic form of communication. He required a system in which the symbol for an item resembled that item. When this change was made to fit existing symbolic capabilities, Kevin's ability to communicate successfully increased significantly.

If a form of symbol is chosen to be used that the individual does not truly understand, it should be noted that the use of the symbol will be limited since it does not reflect deeper competence. In these instances, it must at least be assured that the way in which the person uses the symbol, such as to hand a picture of a hamburger to a waiter, is understood by the partner. In addition, the expectations or goals for the person will focus more on the interaction than on selecting the correct symbol for the interaction. The case study of Ernie, highlighted in Chapter Eight, provides an example of a communication system designed primarily for interactions and sending messages.

3. Successful starts have been made when the vocabulary choices reflect what the individual already knows and what he or she might want to discuss. Just because a set of manufactured pictures includes 100 food items, it cannot be assumed that the individual knows or cares about these items. Just because communication partners want the individual to request "bathroom," it cannot be assumed that the individual shares this wish. The individual's perspective and motivation must be considered when choosing vocabulary.

4. Successful starts have been made when the team recognizes existing signals as legitimate. In other words, the team allows the individual to manipulate them in specific ways with the skills he or she already possesses. There is no need to learn a prerequisite skill, such as switch use,

before the individual is allowed to communicate meaningfully. There is no need to use a symbol for "no" when pushing items away is understood as a rejection. The pushing gesture should be recognized and, if appropriate, a symbol for "no" should be paired with the gesture after the person's existing signal has been legitimized.

5. Successful starts have been made when the individual is empowered as a legitimate communicator who not only is expected to be responsive to others, but also is given opportunities to be an initiator as well. Empowerment is a popular word in terms of parent rights, civil rights, and many social movements in society. It implies that control over every aspect of an individual's life is given to him or her, that he or she is given the power to make decisions and express desires. This should be a feature of all communication systems. Conducting language sessions where an adult holds up an item or picture, labels it, and then requests the individual to also label it is limiting communication to that of only a respondent in an artificial situation.

6. Successful starts have been made when team members remain flexible in their expectations. For example, the beautiful, hand-drawn, colored pictures that the teacher spent 5 hours making might be a flop, thus, he or she may have to resort to another means. Similarly, the lovely oak communication board might be too heavy for the wheelchair, therefore, another means must also be found. Furthermore, not all partners will respond in exactly the same way to the individual's communication signals. Flexibility is the watchword of successful communication systems.

SUMMARY

This chapter contains steps for determining existing communication forms and functions and for ensuring consistency in the use of and response to these signals. The processes of retrospective observation, direct observation, and eliciting particular responses are valid means through which forms, functions, and contexts for communication can be identified. Once identified, consistency in response to these signals must be established. This approach will ensure that the communication system matches the individual's abilities rather than mismatches them.

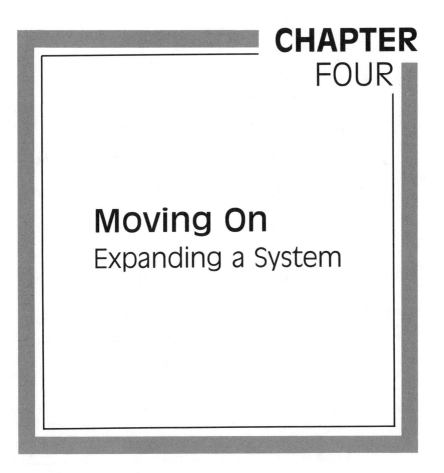

CHAPTER
FOUR

Moving On
Expanding a System

Chapter Three emphasizes the initial aspects of evaluating, designing, and implementing a communication system with some reference to future expansion. The purpose of this chapter is to provide guidelines and additional ideas for the continuing use of augmentative or alternative communication systems with individuals who have moderate to severe disabilities.

WHAT TO EXPAND

Once existing signals are used and acknowledged consistently, the communication system and/or its use may be expanded. Several strategies may be considered as viable options in this process. The particular strategy chosen is dictated by the needs of the individual throughout activities in his or her weekly and daily schedule. The options for expansion include the following:

1. Shaping communication signals to more conventional behavioral forms
2. Changing the symbolic forms to ones that are more readily understood
3. Increasing the number of behavioral and/or symbolic forms
4. Adding new functions for a behavioral and/or symbolic form
5. Introducing new communication partners
6. Selecting additional routines for inclusion in the communication system
7. Decreasing assistance that is needed to use the system

The grid in Appendix A.3 provides a template for expanding communication systems. The emphasis in expansion should be to improve the efficiency of the communication system while decreasing the assistance provided. Communication becomes more efficient when: 1) the forms are more conventional, or easily understood, 2) one form can serve several functions, 3) one function can be expressed through several forms, 4) familiar and unfamiliar partners can use the system with the individual, 5) the system can be used in the context of many daily and less frequent events, and 6) the system can be used with minimal cues, prompts, and assistance in manipulating it. The steps toward achieving this efficiency should be systematic and controlled for complexity. By using this grid, the educational team can remain aware of the demands being placed on the individual for learning new aspects of the system. Each of these aspects is discussed in detail as follows.

Aspect 1: Changing Signals to More Conventional Behavioral Forms

A behavioral form that is more conventional is one that is more easily recognized by members of the individual's cultural community, without specific training. In Chapter Three, the need to identify existing behaviors that could be given communication value is emphasized. The initial behaviors selected, however, are often not conventional in appearance. The use of a more readily understood behavior to communicate would give the individual more opportunities to interact with a larger group of communication partners.

The case study of Ricky, discussed in Chapter Six, provides an example of an attempt at such expansion. Table 4.1 shows the new behavioral form targeted for expansion (see Appendix A.3 for a blank form). The existing behavior form consisted of looking at the desired item and touching it in order to request that item. An even clearer form is touching while alternating gaze between the item and the person who can get it. The teacher planned to shape alternating gaze within the existing snack routine by bringing the item close to her face after Ricky had looked at it and touched it. By inserting a delay in delivering the item, the teacher found that Ricky would look at her briefly in a puzzled manner. When he did, she delivered the item immediately. In this manner, she demonstrated that this additional behavior led to the speedy delivery of the desired item and was, thus, more efficient. While the demand for this new behavior was gradually increased, Ricky's old system of gaze and touch was allowed to continue to work as a back-up if he failed to respond to the use of the new system with alternating gaze. This effort was abandoned, however, for cultural reasons discussed in his case study.

Aspect 2: Changing the Symbolic Form

The symbolic form is the representation used as a code for the meaning of the message. Symbolic forms may be quite abstract, such as words, manual signs, or line drawings. They may even closely resemble the item referred to, as with photographs or colored catalog pictures. The forms may also be quite obvious in meaning, using miniatures, actual objects, or realistic replicas of the objects.

At least two scenarios are possible with individuals who

Table 4.1.   Example of expanding the behavioral form using the grid for expanding communication systems

Aspects	Existing[a]	New[b]
Behavioral form	(Describe)	
Vocal		
Verbal		
Gestural	Touch object	Touch object
Gaze	Look at object	Look at object and at adult
Other		
Symbolic form	(Describe appearance and/or list)	
Real objects	Cracker and drink	
Replicas		
Miniatures		
Photos		
Pictures		
Other		
Function of signal	(Describe specific function in each category[c])	
Behavioral regulation	Request food item	
Social interaction		
Joint activity		
Communication partner	(List names and familiarity with system user)	
Person: Familiar/ unfamiliar	Teacher: Familiar	
Environment/activity/context	(List by category)	
Daily	Snack	
Weekly		
Monthly		
Other		
Assistance	(Describe type)	
Natural cues/prompts		
Frequency		
Instructional cues/prompts	Present two items, pause	Same, but move item toward face, pause
Frequency	100% of the time	

[a]Existing = currently used

[b]New = changed

[c]See Wetherby and Prizant (1989)

Table 4.2. Example of expanding the symbolic form using the grid for expanding communication systems

Aspects	Existing[a]	New[b]
Behavioral form	(Describe)	
Vocal		
Verbal		
Gestural	Point to object	
Gaze	Look at object	
Other		
Symbolic form	(Describe appearance and/or list)	
Real objects	Comb, toothbrush	
Replicas		
Miniatures		Comb, toothbrush
Photos		
Pictures		
Other		
Function of signal	(Describe specific function in each category[c])	
Behavioral regulation	Request object	
Social interaction		
Joint activity	Comment	
Communication partner	(List names and familiarity with system user)	
Person: Familiar/ unfamiliar	Parent: Familiar Teacher: Familiar	
Environment/activity/context	(List by category)	
Daily	Grooming	
Weekly		
Monthly		
Other		
Assistance	(Describe type)	
Natural cues/prompts		
Frequency		
Instructional cues/prompts	Present miniatures with objects underneath, pause	
Frequency	100% of the time	

[a]Existing = currently used

[b]New = changed

[c]See Wetherby and Prizant (1989)

have moderate to severe disabilities with regard to symbolic form. First, an individual may have the potential to learn the representative value of the more abstract symbols mentioned. In this case, gradual changes from the more obvious or iconic forms to more abstract forms are targeted in successive steps. Table 4.2 illustrates one step in such a change (see Appendix A.3 for a blank form).

The second scenario might involve an individual who may be slow to develop representational skills and yet has a variety of needs for communication. The case history of Ernie, described in Chapter Eight, provides such an example. A photograph was used to order fast food in restaurants. The symbol itself was meaningful to the restaurant worker, whereas, the act of using the symbol was meaningful to Ernie because it was a tool to reach a desired goal. He learned to use this symbol, and later, others, in specific situations with a variety of partners. Although he may not have understood the usual meaning of the symbolic representation, he learned when and where to use the method in order to interact successfully with peers and other adults.

Sometimes, changes in the symbolic form occur without specific planning. The individual may discover a form that others understand by accident. For example, Jenny, who is visually and hearing impaired, was crawling around her leisure space one day and found a metal tube on the floor. She held it up, vocalized, and headed toward the bathroom. When she arrived, she reached up for the metal bar surrounding the toilet, dropping the metal tube. An aide, who had observed this, suggested that the metal tube be added to Jenny's object board. Jenny immediately began to use it to request "bathroom." This highlights the need to consider the individual's perspective and meanings when expanding the system.

Aspect 3: Increasing the Number of Behavioral or Symbolic Forms

Increasing the number of forms used by the individual is the same as expanding his or her vocabulary. By examining familiar routines, it may become evident that the individual has been exposed to common vocabulary and that he or she might want to express some of these forms. In this instance, additional forms could be used to express a more specific choice. For example, instead of "drink," the individual might want to choose "coffee" or "soda."

When these new forms are added, they should serve existing functions. In other words, the new form should represent another means to achieve a familiar communication goal. Donny, for example, used vocalizations to request continued action such as rocking or swinging. It was noticed that he often lifted his arms slightly in anticipation of being lifted up. It was decided that "arms up" would be a new form for requesting that the adult continue the motion of picking him up. The adult would come near Donny with hands in position for picking him up and pause with hands firmly under Donny's armpits, lifting slightly. When Donny lifted his arms, he was using a new signal to request continuation.

Aspect 4: Adding New Functions

Using Wetherby's and Prizant's (1989) or Dore's (1974, 1975) listing of functions, presented in Chapter Two, an individual's existing forms can be examined for the variety of functions served. In Table 4.3, the behavioral form of vocalizing and looking at the adult was used for requesting more of a social routine (see Appendix A.3 for a blank form). It was decided that the same behavioral form would serve the function of requesting more of a food substance to make the form more versatile. The only other aspect that was altered was the routine. As mentioned, the more functions a single form can serve, the more efficient the communication system.

Aspect 5: Increasing the Number of Communication Partners

Often, individuals, such as those in the case histories, have a limited number of communication partners who can under-

Table 4.3. Example of expanding the functions using the grid for expanding communication systems

Aspects	Existing[a]	New[b]
Behavioral form	(Describe)	
Vocal	"Uhhh" or "mmmm"	
Verbal		
Gestural		
Gaze	Look at partner	
Other		
Symbolic form	(Describe appearance and/or list)	
Real objects		
Replicas		
Miniatures		
Photos		
Pictures		
Other	None	
Function of signal	(Describe specific function in each category[c])	
Behavioral regulation		
Social interaction	Request for more of a social routine	Request more of substance
Joint activity		
Communication partner	(List names and familiarity with system user)	
Person: Familiar/ unfamiliar	Teacher: Familiar	
Environment/activity/context	(List by category)	
Daily	Rocking, swinging	Snack
Weekly		
Monthly		
Other		
Assistance	(Describe type)	
Natural cues/prompts		
Frequency		
Instructional cues/prompts	Pause routine	Pause giving snack
Frequency	Four times per routine	

[a]Existing = currently used
[b]New = changed
[c]See Wetherby and Prizant (1989)

stand their communication attempts. This may be due to the character of the signals—they may not be readily understood by less familiar partners. If this is the case, an effort should be made to train new partners to identify the signal and respond appropriately. As mentioned in Chapter Three, training might include modeling or watching videotapes of a more skilled partner who is interacting with the individual.

Another limiting factor in the number of partners is the setting. Domestic and educational settings might be more controlled than usual for a variety of reasons. A side effect is that few outside persons come in contact with the user of the augmentative or alternative communication system. In these instances, a specific effort should be made to increase the individual's number of partners and interactions. For example, the cook at a high school served lunch to all of the students including the individuals with disabilities. The cook was usually in a hurry to finish serving all the students on time. Three students had augmentative communication systems that included food choices, but they had not been able to use the system in the lunchroom. It was arranged that these three students would come early until they and the cook became efficient with the systems. The teacher made symbols available for the possible food choices ahead of time and trained the cook through modeling. The cook reported that he was surprised that these three students "had so much to say."

A reality of working in public programs is that the turnover rate of professionals is high. Although this may be a continuing dilemma, the educational team can anticipate the problem and design an instructional plan that can be implemented at any time of the year. Photographs, videotapes, and modeling can be used to convey the character of the system. One of the more stable members of the educational team, usually the parent or teacher, could be designated as the instructor for new partners.

One last consideration regarding partners is the need for peer interaction. In some respects, individuals with moderate to severe disabilities learn to interact only with adult caregivers due to the types of opportunities made available. Adults have often designed the system and/or are the only partners instructed in the system. An effort should be directed at increasing the opportunities for the individual to interact with peers or siblings by providing instruction to these partners as well.

Aspect 6: Using the System in New Contexts

Being able to communicate in all settings is the ultimate goal for any communicator. When an augmentative or alternative communication system is first tried, its use may be limited to one or two events in the day. Once the individual understands and uses the system in these contexts, other events can be added. This does not imply that completely new activities must be designed for using the system. Instead, examine the existing events in the individual's day and determine ways in which to use the system during these events. Some activities may offer many opportunities for expressing choices (e.g., leisure time, grooming, meals), whereas others offer opportunities to give information (e.g., structured learning activities, morning sharing time). For some individuals, it will be possible to expand their communication system into all of these activities such that they become an active participant in each event.

Aspect 7: Decreasing Assistance for Using the System

The goal for an individual who needs a communication system is to make it as functional and efficient as possible. This implies independent use of his or her system. Although some individuals may never be totally independent, systematic considerations should be given to decreasing the frequency of assistance and to making the type of assistance less reliant on obvious cues or prompts. Tactile plus verbal cues can be faded to verbal-only cues that can, in turn, change to environmental cues.

Most practitioners are well-versed in these behavioral methods. However, there remains a need to reduce the emphasis on adult and/or instructional cues for communication.

Duchan (1983) and Halle (1985), and others discuss the predominance of teacher- or adult-initiated interactions with individuals who do not communicate proficiently without assistance. This high level of adult initiations can result in a low level of assertiveness on the part of the individual who learns to rely on the adult to begin conversing. By systematically emphasizing natural cues and correction procedures, professionals can enable the individual to become an active rather than passive communicator. This, in turn, increases his or her effectiveness with the system.

EXAMINING PROBLEMS WITH THE SYSTEM

Whether you are getting started or moving on, it is necessary to remain flexible when expanding the communication system and solving problems that arise. Often, a key factor is overlooked that blocks further development and use of a system. Some of these factors have already been discussed, such as the high rate of adult-initiated interactions leading to or encouraging a respondent-only role on the individual's part.

Another common problem expressed by many caregivers and teachers is that the individual does not seem motivated to use the communication system. Two factors should be examined in this case: the individual's awareness of his or her ability to manipulate others through communication, and the functions and contexts for using the system. The first factor is addressed in Chapter Two. The second factor might become clearer when an analysis of form and function is conducted. If a system is not providing the individual with some sense of control over the actions of others, it will remain unused. A system that is only used in mass trial training for recognition of pictures is not a communication system. Using a system for requesting during routines might be a first step in remedying this situation.

Another related factor is the physical ability of the individual to manipulate his or her communication system. Perhaps the positioning is such that the individual's trunk is unstable, preventing him or her from pointing to objects accurately. Visual scanning and tracking abilities, discussed in Chapter Five, may be the source of difficulty as well. Obviously, team involvement in the expansion and use of the communication system will assist in examining the individual's problems from many perspectives.

SUCCESSFUL SYSTEMS

The case histories in the following chapters contain examples of communication systems that continue to be used successfully. The common elements of these systems are as follows:

1. Many of the partners were willing to use the system to facilitate communication with the individual. (In some cases, not all of the partners were involved in designing the system.)
2. The communication systems were designed to be flexible in order to allow for adjustments as the individual's needs changed.
3. More than one communication format was implemented. Some individuals used more than one behavioral or symbolic form to convey meaning (e.g., pictures, vocalizations).
4. As teachers and other professionals change, the parent or caregiver becomes the primary instructor for the use and expansion of the system. This has been more successful when the parent and caregiver have had considerable input into the design and use of the system and when their preferences are reflected in it.
5. The partners were keen observers, recognizing the communicative intent or value of subtle and unconventional behaviors.
6. Those involved in designing the system were highly motivated, creative, and flexible enough to try another way. The commitment to providing a means of communication

to individuals with disabilities has been the ultimate motivator.

SUMMARY

This chapter contains guidelines and additional ideas to assist in the continued use and expansion of a communication system. The template presented and explained in the chapter can direct efforts of interventionists to the critical aspects for continued use and expansion, *and* focus efforts so the number and type of new things taught is not unrealistic (too much or too little). The information will help ensure that the system is used, expansion occurs, communication partners and interventionists coordinate efforts, and exchanges and planning occur so the system is not "lost" as personnel turnover occurs.

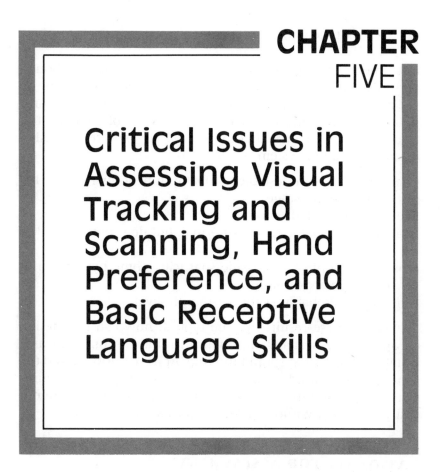

CHAPTER
FIVE

Critical Issues in Assessing Visual Tracking and Scanning, Hand Preference, and Basic Receptive Language Skills

A communication system can often be the key to many activities, environments, and relationships for people with disabilities. While there are many communication systems available, each must be tailored to the needs of the user. Part of this "tailoring" involves an understanding of the skills that are relevant to communicative functioning for an individual with severe disabilities. At minimum, the following areas of functioning should be assessed prior to the development of an appropriate communication system: cognition, motor functioning, sensory abilities, speech and language, and current and future communication needs of the individual (Musselwhite & St. Louis, 1982; Silverman, 1980). While many standardized

This chapter has been authored by Brent A. Askvig, M.S. (doctoral candidate), Department of Counseling and Special Education, University of Idaho, Moscow.

instruments provide educators with some information about a person's skills and deficits in these areas, they frequently do not provide information detailed enough to develop an appropriate communication system. Educators are often given test results such as the ones that follow and are expected to design a communication system:

Cognition: IQ—untestable; probably functioning in the 12- to 18-month range

Speech: No verbal speech

Hearing: Tympanic reflexes normal, but does not respond to name

Motor Functioning: Left side spasticity; some hypertonia in right upper extremity

Language: Probably at the 12-month level

While these results may be typical, how can one design an appropriate system? How will the student communicate? What kind of system should the student have? How should the system be organized? About what will the student communicate? Where will the system be used? These questions are not easily answered without further information.

RATIONALE FOR ASSESSMENT

This chapter is intended to be used as a guide in assessing some of the skills that are critical when using augmentative and alternative communication systems. In particular, the chapter focuses on assessing visual tracking and scanning abilities, hand preference, and basic receptive language skills as they apply to the planning and development of communication systems for students with severe disabilities. Although there are other abilities that must be assessed (e.g., cognition, hearing, positioning, reach, grasp), resources for assessing these skills are more abundant than the information that is presented here. A resource list for assessment information on gross and fine motor skills, cognition, pragmatics, and current and future ecological factors is provided at the end of this chapter. In addition, the list contains resources on instructional strategies and augmentative and alternative communication systems and materials. The reason for emphasizing tracking, scanning, hand preference, and basic receptive language skills is that there is little information readily available about how to assess these abilities, since this information is often "new" to many practitioners. However, these skills are critical when using most communication systems, whether they are teacher-developed or commercially made. Too frequently, communication systems are placed where the user cannot reach the symbols, cannot clearly see the materials , or cannot visually scan all the possible symbol options available. This often results in frustration, teacher disappointment, and a strong possibility that an appropriate system will not be developed.

For each of the skills of visual tracking, visual scanning, hand preference, and receptive language, a rationale and some possible methods for assessing these skills for use with communication systems are presented. The methods given are only some of the possible ways to assess these skills. For each individual, adjustments may need to be made in the amount of time spent in assessing, the materials used, and the assessment location. For example, in the case histories in this book, daily routines are often used to gather data on these skills. Before discussing the specific assessment procedures, however, there are several general considerations regarding the assessment of individuals with severe disabilities that should be discussed.

GENERAL CONSIDERATIONS

First, have someone familiar with the individual conduct the assessment. This will speed up the assessment process considerably as teacher-learner rapport will already have been established. For example, the teacher or parent/caregiver will usually know which times of the day the student will respond best, what motivates the student, and whether his or her responses are typical or atypical of the general abilities. However, it is good practice to have another person verify the information that is obtained or the conclusions drawn about the learner's performance to make sure that they are reliable. This is necessary as observer expectations may bias what is observed and result in incorrect conclusions about performance and potential teaching strategies.

Second, whenever possible, assess in natural settings and typical daily routines. This includes using familiar activities in the classroom, at home, and in the community. For instance, if a student shows an interest in watching other students at recess, this is a good time to structure visual tracking or scanning skills by having peers walk across the playground in various ways so as to test tracking, or by having the student visually scan a section of the playground for a certain friend.

Third, use materials and activities or routines about which the person already communicates and is familiar. It is important to determine if a person is familiar with activities or materials before expecting him or her to communicate about them. This is especially important in assessment situations since novel experiences can often result in atypical responses when the learner attempts to assimilate the new information. The end result is that the learner's responses are not true indicators of performance. For example, one student was being assessed for visual tracking skills during an art activity in the classroom. The examiner was using various art materials (e.g., large brushes, different sheets of colored paper) as stimuli for the tracking. The student appeared to be doing well until the examiner held up a macrame mask that another student had made. The mask was new to the student and frightened her, causing her to turn her head away and quit tracking. This reaction was an indication of the student's emotions rather than her inability to visually track.

Fourth, use preferred and nonpreferred objects at various points in the assessment. Use of preferred objects can facilitate the person's motivation and attention during the assessment process. However, the evaluator should be wary of the effects of pairing items that are highly preferred with those that are not. For example, one 3-year-old really enjoyed playing with toy cars. Whenever a toy car was presented during the assessment with the request to chose one of two toys that were placed in front of him (e.g., car or ball), he always chose the car. The test results indicated that he did not understand the words since he always picked up the car. Subsequent testers found (without using the favorite toy) that he understood 25 other words! Thus, while the toy was certainly motivating to the student, it also interfered with his ability to demonstrate his skills. Using two objects of approximately the same preference may help to solve this problem. That is, if the learner enjoys some materials equally well, then use those together, rather than pairing them with less (or more) preferred items.

Finally, adjust the presentation of the stimulus materials to the abilities of the individual. The speed of item presentation, the size of the materials, reinforcers used, and the time of day may all influence performance. For instance, a learner with motoric deficits may give more accurate responses early in the day, while another person may give more accurate responses after he or she has had a coffee or lunch break. Similarly, if the learner is visually impaired, initially use large brightly colored objects, followed by smaller and less stimulating ones. Again, an examiner who is familiar with the individual will be able to adjust the assessment for the unique needs of that person.

VISUAL ASSESSMENT

This section describes some methods for assessing visual tracking and scanning abilities of persons with severe disabilities. While recognizing that there are other visual functions that are important, such as visual fixation and focusing, this chapter is limited to tracking and scanning abilities and their applications to communication systems. These skills are chosen for discussion because they are so critical to the use of alternative and augmentative communication systems. A person with such a system will generally be expected to utilize tracking and scanning in a number of ways, such as searching for a symbol on a communication board (i.e., scanning), watching a person with whom he or she is communicating move across the room, or following a teacher's pointing, and other gestures that give direction (i.e., tracking). It should be noted that these assessment procedures are not meant to assess other visual impairments. If the student has visual deficits, consultation with an ophthalmologist or other vision specialist regarding limitations of these problems is suggested. The visual assessment conducted by the teacher or other personnel should provide specific information regarding the visual strengths and deficits of the individual. For instance, if a person has strabismus or uses only peripheral vision, the assessment can help school personnel determine where to place objects and how to maximize abilities.

Visual Tracking

Visual tracking is the ability to follow an object or person as it moves through a number of visual planes (Scheuerman, Baumgart, Sipsma, & Brown, 1976). Smooth, consistent tracking is essential because it allows a person to observe the environment efficiently. These observations will frequently be the basis for the events or objects about which an individual will communicate. Also, since people rarely sit still (especially children), tracking allows one to maintain visual contact before, during, and after interactions. Knowing a person's limitations in visually following people or objects (e.g., speed of movement, optimum location in the visual field) allows one to design a communication system that takes advantage of the person's visual strengths and does not penalize him or her for visual deficits.

Visual Planes   There are several planes on which a person may visually track objects. Generally, these planes are the vertical plane, the horizontal plane, and the diagonal planes. For each plane, there are at least two directions that the objects may move in the visual field. The typical point of reference for movement in the visual field is called midpoint. This is the point directly in front of the person's face at eye level. In the vertical plane, objects may move from the top of the visual field to the bottom, above eye level to below eye level, and in the reverse direction. In the horizontal plane, objects may move from left to right or from right to left. In the more complex diagonal planes, objects may move from the upper right visual field location to the lower left (or the reverse) and, similarly, from the upper left to the lower right (or the reverse). In addition, objects may move in random directions where there is no apparent pattern of movement. The visual assessment forms in the Appendix (see Appendix A.4) clearly specifies these planes and movements.

Musselwhite and St. Louis (1982) list several considerations for assessing visual tracking. Specifically, they note that the size, shape, and color of the objects used; the visual field location; the distance of the objects from the person; the cue(s) used; the speed and path of the objects; and the barriers for shielding objects all can affect the ability to track efficiently. They suggest systematically manipulating each of these variables to test their effect on the individual's tracking. In addition, lighting in the room, foreground/background contrast, and the presence of other visually distracting items in the visual field can affect tracking ability. These latter factors are especially important with persons with visual impairments.

Procedure Several early childhood assessment instruments contain visual tracking items that might be helpful in assessing tracking (e.g., Bayley Scales of Infant Development [Bayley, 1969]). For example, there are several items on the Bayley that assess an infant's ability to visually follow a light, a red ring, or a ball. Also, Erhardt (1986) has developed an instrument for assessing the visual functions of infants and young children. However, these instruments are developmentally based and their use with older individuals with moderate or severe handicaps is not addressed. Furthermore, they were not designed to gather information with respect to functional communication systems. Visual tracking can easily be assessed through more informal methods by having the individual watch an object as it moves through the visual planes. It is important that the person be comfortably positioned, preferably sitting, if there are no apparent motor difficulties. When individuals with severe disabilities have motor or muscle imbalances, such as cerebral palsy, a physical or occupational therapist must be consulted about correct positioning since it affects head control. Both motor or muscle balance and head control are critical to smooth tracking. Persons with poor head control may have to be placed in seemingly unusual positions for assessment, such as lying on the floor or sitting on the lap of another person to assess their "best" abilities. A comfortable and stable head position is important.

For individuals with suspected visual problems, brightly colored objects with distinct shapes and edges will help them visually locate the items. Also, variations in room lighting or a contrasting background and foreground can assist the individual in visually locating and tracking objects. For example, lighted objects (e.g., a small pen flashlight, a glow-in-the-dark toy) in a darkened room have been observed to produce tracking and head control in a person previously believed to have neither skill.

Visual tracking can be assessed in an informal manner in many natural daily activities. There are several instances when situations can be structured for such an assessment. For example, Joshua, a young adult with severe physical impairments and mental retardation, required an assistant to feed him due to the lack of functional hand use. The assistant incorporated several mealtime activities to assess Joshua's visual tracking abilities. For instance, once the assistant had seated Joshua at the table she told him to watch her as she set the table, moving slowly from left to right and right to left along the table, opposite where he was sitting. The assistant also placed the ketchup bottle on the end of the table and, when Joshua needed the ketchup, she had the people on the opposite side of the table pass the ketchup bottle to him as she prompted Joshua to watch.

Visual tracking can also be assessed in a more formal manner by using a repeated trials format. Begin by showing the person a preferred object, one that he or she will watch as it is moved. Position the object at eye level to either the left or right side of the person, approximately 12–18 inches away from the nose. If necessary, shake or tap the item to get the person's attention. Then slowly (e.g., 3–4 inches per second) move the object horizontally across the person's field of vision, carefully monitoring his or her eye movements. Repeat this procedure for horizontal tracking, both 6–8 inches above and below eye level, and for vertical and diagonal tracking. A form to facilitate data collection on visual tracking using either of the above methods is provided in the Appendix (see Appendix A.4). Actual visual tracking data using these methods is shown in the case history of Kyle in Chapter Seven.

While assessing tracking abilities, note whether the person's eyes move in a smooth, continuous motion, or whether they move in a jerky, interrupted fashion. Eye movements in a jerky up and down or side to side direction, or eye(s) turning in or out may be noted in some individuals. These movements can be indicative of nystagmus (i.e., oscillating movement of the eyeballs) or strabismus (i.e., eyes that turn in or out). These conditions may require the objects to be moved at slower speeds than would normally be used. Other factors to consider are whether the eyes move together when tracking, where the person begins the tracking (e.g., at the periphery of the visual field, at midline), and if the individual appears to fatigue as the session progresses. For example, persons with only peripheral vision will not be able to "see," scan, or track objects in their central field of vision. It is important to determine where their peripheral field of vision begins and ends to accurately determine placement of items.

Use of the Results The results from the visual tracking assessment are helpful in selecting an appropriate communication system. The assessment allows documentation of the individual's tracking skills: which directions the person can track, consistency of eye gaze during tracking, the preferred or "best" visual field, and potential inhibitors to smooth tracking (e.g., erratic eye movements, poor head mobility). With some persons, smooth visual tracking may be observed in only one plane, in one quadrant, or in scattered portions of their visual field. For example, one former student did not track objects vertically and could not smoothly track past midline in either the horizontal or diagonal planes. The assessment results indicated that the area in which he could most easily track and visually observe and/or scan objects was in the upper left visual field, approximately 18 inches away from his eyes. Subsequently, objects were presented visually to him in that area. Objects placed before him on a table (a typical occurance) were quite difficult for him to observe.

Knowledge of the above factors helps to determine the most appropriate placement of objects or symbols in the person's visual field, whether or not the symbols or objects may need to be highlighted (e.g., made brighter by adding color, using contrasting foreground and background colors), and whether or not the speed of presentation of visual stimuli (e.g., objects, communication symbols) should be slowed or increased. For example, if the individual has peripheral vision only, communication symbols may have to be placed around the edge of a communication board, or extra time allowed for the person to reposition his or her head to adequately view the necessary symbols or person with whom he or she is communicating.

Visual Scanning

Visual scanning is the ability to search for parts of an object or to inspect an array of objects (Scheuerman et al., 1976). Essentially, scanning involves the ability to search for and to voluntarily stop and visually select a component part of the object or one item in a series of objects that is being examined. It is a more complex task than visual tracking and is a critical skill for many alternative and augmentative communication systems. Many systems require the user to visually scan a series of symbols or words and then select (e.g., by looking at, pointing to) the desired symbol. For example, a student who utilized a series of miniature items placed in a row according to the daily classroom routine might use the following sequence of visual skills:

Visually locate set of miniature objects
Scan (from left to right) the set of objects for the item representing the next activity

Visually fixate on and pick up (or point to) the desired object

Typically, scanning follows a left to right, top to bottom sequence of movement. However, this may not be the most efficient pattern for some persons. The author recalls a student with severe cerebral palsy who utilized a right to left scan for his communication board. Severe muscle spasticity prevented this student from adequately controlling his head for left to right movements, or crossing midline when moving from the right. However, he could scan from right to left, beginning at midline and moving to his left. His communication board was constructed such that all items were placed to the left of midline. Also, the nouns were placed on the right side of the symbol set, with the verbs in the middle and the adjectives and adverbs on the left side. Although this was exactly opposite of how most systems are arranged, it worked wonderfully for this person.

Procedure   Visual scanning can be assessed in a number of different ways. For example, the individual being assessed could be shown a picture with several objects on it and asked to locate specific items on that picture. Another way might be to have a student locate a specific object in the classroom, such as another student or certain classroom materials. It is often difficult to observe a person's eye movements as he or she attempts to scan the larger environment; therefore, scanning is often assessed in a more clinical type of setting. Then, once the person's scanning abilities have been documented in a structured setting, they may be observed in more natural situations.

For a more formal assessment procedure, begin by seating the person at a table or large desk, making sure there are few distractions. Arrange to have one person manipulate the items and have a second person observe eye movements and record data. The two observers can then confirm the person's eye movements, if necessary. Other arrangements may be necessary if the individual has unique positioning needs, such as lying on his or her side or standing with supportive equipment. Select at least 8 items that the person is familiar with and will want to look at and use after a portion or all of the assessment has been completed. Favorite toys or classroom materials (e.g., books, games) are some items that may work for students. Place the items in various positions within the person's visual field (see Appendix A.4 for some possible positions). For instance, place one object slightly to the front and left of the individual, one object directly in front, and another object to the front and right. While placing the objects, observe the individual's eyes. Note whether he or she shifts the gaze from item to item in a smooth fashion or looks past the object and then returns to it. Observe if the individual begins searching for objects at a particular place in his or her visual field. Finally, watch for a pattern in the visual search. Some people may begin searching in the upper left of their visual field and move across the field in an up and down scanning motion, while others look from left to right or the reverse across their visual field and move from the top to bottom. Some people will use no identifiable scanning pattern, and some are able to select the correct item without visibly "looking."

For those individuals who may be able to use a communication board, another type of scanning assessment procedure may be useful. Arrange the items in a row or an array in front of the person. Figure 5.1 shows some suggested arrangements of items for scanning three, four, six, or eight items. (Note: Positioning of the objects and the number of objects used may need to be adjusted depending upon the results of the visual tracking assessment and the person's cognitive/discrimination abilities. For example, if the individual only tracks objects to the left side of his or her body, it would not be appropriate to expect the individual to scan on his or her right side.) Then, ask the person to "find" a specific item. This may be done by having the student pick up the object, point to it, or look at it. For those individuals who cannot choose one item from two or more different ones (i.e., discrimination), scanning may be assessed by using two or more objects that are the same. Again, while the person is visually searching the array of objects, monitor his or her eye movements. Does he or she first look to one specific area each time? Do his or her eyes wander randomly from item to item or is there a specific pattern in the visual search? What is the pattern? A visual scanning data

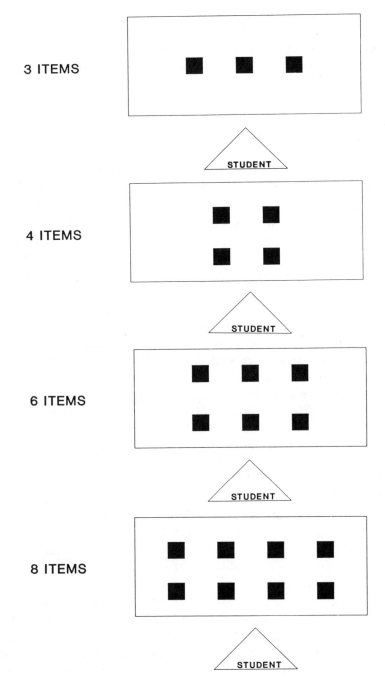

Figure 5.1. Arrangements of items for visual scanning assessment.

sheet is provided in the Appendix (see Appendix A.5) and lists some of the critical behaviors that should be monitored during the scanning assessment. Repeat the procedure several times, alternating the position of the objects each time. Also, repeat the procedure using four, six, eight, or more items as appropriate for the individual.

It is useful to confirm a person's scanning skills through natural observation or activities that are structured during the daily routine. This can be accomplished by systematically observing the person's visual scanning skills in several daily activities such as looking at a book (e.g., Does he or she scan the pages or the pictures?), looking at the choices for clothing to wear, or searching a shelf or work area for materials for the next classroom or work activity. An example of a structured natural routine would be to place two coats next to the person's coat on a rack. Then, when it is time to get his or her coat after work, the person must scan across all of the coats on the rack to find his or her own. As with the other methods of scanning assessment, record the starting point of the search and the pattern of scanning.

Use of the Results   Visual scanning skills are critical for using many different communication systems. The results from the scanning assessment will aid in deciding upon the appropriate layout and format of the system. In particular, the teacher or therapist will know: how to place the system in the visual field to maximize visual contact; the number of objects or symbols the person can efficiently scan and, thus, use in the system; and how to arrange the symbols or objects to match the person's scanning pattern. Finally, by varying the size of the materials used during the scanning assessment, one can determine the most appropriate size of symbols or objects for the individual's system. In Chapter Seven, Jodi's visual scanning and tracking abilities are assessed as described here. The results indicated that she could efficiently track from left to right, and scan a series of eight or more items from left to right as long as they were not above her eye level. Her schedule system was then designed such that she had no more than six or seven items to scan. Also, it was placed on a low table so that she could more easily see the items.

HAND PREFERENCE ASSESSMENT

Assessment of hand preference is the determination of the dominant hand with which the person reaches for, points to, and/or grasps objects. Prior to age 6 or 7, a child may not have established a dominant hand and may use either equally well. In some cases, physical disabilities may limit or inhibit a person's use of a hand or arm. Hand preference is assessed so that teachers and therapists can design communication systems that allow easy access for the user. One must know the limitations of the pointing and reaching and must know whether or not the individual can reach to and across midline.

Procedure Hand preference should be assessed in both the sitting and standing positions, if possible. For each position, place an object successively at each of the following locations in relation to the front of the individual: left-forward, left-side, forward, middle, right-forward, and right-side (see Appendix A.6, the Data Sheet for Assessing Hand Preference, for the specific locations). In the sitting position, the objects should be placed on a table top or desk for easiest access. When standing, the items should be held approximately at the person's chest level. Adjust the items as necessary for individual differences in positioning or visual abilities. Allow the person to reach for and get the item at each location and record which hand he or she uses to get it. If necessary, use verbal or gestural prompts to facilitate a response. During the assessment, note whether the person uses the same hand when the item is to the left of midline, at midline, and to the right of midline. Does he or she use the same hand for every reach? Does he or she use the left hand for items placed to the left of midline and the right hand when items are placed to the right of midline? A form for recording hand preference assessment results is provided in the Appendix (see Appendix A.6).

For some individuals, the hand preference assessment procedure can be completed in 5–10 minutes. For those persons with motor problems, however, it may take considerably longer. Many times favorite objects can stimulate reflexive movements that will inhibit smooth reach and grasp. Also, changes in muscle tone or the need for frequent repositioning may prolong the assessment and cause frustration or fatigue. In these instances, the assessment can be completed in several sessions throughout several days or even weeks. In addition, some students may not exhibit a strong preference for either hand, even during many trials. However, do not be alarmed, as the student may be ambidextrous or may develop hand dominance at a later date.

Use of the Results The results of the hand preference assessment provide valuable information for designing and constructing a communication system. First, the hand a person is likely to use in manipulating objects (and, subsequently, to use for a communication system) is identified. However, exclusive use of the preferred hand can be beneficial or a hindrance, depending upon the system used. For example, one child not only demonstrated a strong right hand preference but had very weak control and strength in his left hand. He used a communication booklet with line drawings on $2\frac{1}{2}$ inch by 4 inch cards placed in plastic holders in a small binder and had very little difficulty turning the pages with his right hand and using the appropriate cards. However, he became frustrated by the amount of time it took him to use the booklet when eating. Since he was right handed, he had to put down his spoon, grasp his booklet, and then turn the pages of his booklet to locate the appropriate symbol for his message. But this was not fast enough for him. He tried several alternative methods (such as using his messy spoon to turn the pages) before deciding that anything he wanted to say could wait until he had finished eating.

Second, the hand preference assessment provides information about the person's reaching abilities, specifically his or her ability to cross midline. Although it is not an upper extremity mobility test, it does allow the observer to note those areas that the individual can most easily reach. This is important when considering placement of the communication system and other stimuli for instruction. For example, if the person has a dominant left hand, cannot cross midline while reaching with the left hand, and cannot use his or her right hand at all, materials must be placed on the left side.

Finally, the examiner can observe differences in hand preference in both the sitting and standing positions. Sometimes young children and others with balance and mobility problems use their preferred hand to assist in steadying themselves. If the teacher or therapist is considering a communication system that requires both hands or that must be carried, the person may be unable to efficiently use it in some sitting or standing positions. One solution to this problem is to have the individual sit each time he or she has to use the system. However, the teacher will have to take this into consideration when planning instructional activities, especially those that require extensive movement and communication. Consultation with a physical or occupational therapist is also helpful in these situations.

BASIC RECEPTIVE LANGUAGE ASSESSMENT

Receptive language is the "ability to understand speech and nonverbal (gestural) communication" (Silverman, 1980, p. 180). It is important to differentiate the assessment of basic receptive language and other similar skills such as item discrimination and functional object use. Item discrimination requires the individual to observe two or more objects and to determine which ones are the "same" or "different." Functional object use requires the person to use an item correctly in the appropriate manner, (e.g., drink from a glass, push a shopping cart, put on a shoe). In each case, a verbal command or request may or may not be used. In the assessment of basic receptive language skills, the person is given a verbal request (with and without gestures) to perform a movement, act upon an object, or interact with another person. In essence, an individual must comprehend what another person has said and the tester must determine if comprehension occurs only with gestures, without the gestures, and whether the context assists in comprehension. This section presents several ways of assessing basic receptive language skills.

Procedure Several formal assessment instruments have been used, with varying success, to determine the receptive language abilities of persons with severe handicaps. Two popular instruments are the Peabody Picture Vocabulary Test (PPVT) (Dunn, 1965) and the Test for Auditory Comprehension of Language (TACL) (Carrow, 1973). However, limitations in student abilities, unfamiliar vocabulary, and testing arrangements often preclude use of these instruments for persons with severe disabilities. A different approach has been to use more criterion-referenced measures, such as two choice discrimination tasks, that have been judged to be at least as reliable as some standardized instruments in determining general receptive language abilities (Pecyna & Sommers, 1985). The criterion-referenced approach is useful because, unlike many of the more formal, standardized instruments, testing situations can be modified to include vocabulary, materials, and activities familiar to the student. Also, alternative responses such as eye pointing, vocalizations, or eye blinks are allowed. The methods described below are all criterion-referenced, and adjustments should be made to accommodate individual differences. However, even using these procedures, there often remain doubts about the person's abilities.

Basic Receptive Language Skills Naturalistic observation is used to begin assessing receptive language skills. This is done by asking the student to obtain familiar objects or to look at familiar people as events naturally occur throughout the day. For example, as a student enters a classroom, hand him or her an item and ask him or her to give it to a teacher or a classmate. Likewise have numerous items on a shelf, such as a book, pen, or cup, and ask him or her to get a certain item. Keep a list of the persons and objects named, along with the student's responses, to obtain a list of current receptive vocabulary in familiar contexts.

Also, an individual's comprehension of simple one- or two-step commands can be examined during typical daily activities. For instance, in a work setting, the following situation can be structured to assess comprehension of one step directions both with and without gestural cues. During work, ask the person to pick up an object. On one occasion, point to the object while asking the person to pick it up, and on another occasion, omit the pointing. Carefully observe the person's response and record the situation, cues provided (i.e., verbal, gestural), and the individual's response on the data collection form shown in the Appendix (see Appendix A.7). The key factors in this assessment are to: 1) keep the directions or requests simple at first (e.g., "Get cup," "Come here," "Sit down"), and then later progress to more complex directions; 2) systematically vary the use or exclusion of gestures as additional cues to the subject; and 3) provide directions in typical and atypical settings or routines, and carefully record the setting of the assessment, the cues provided, and the person's response.

In addition, an individual's understanding of many nonverbal forms of communication can be assessed by using gestures and body movements. Some familiar gestures to use are waving hello and good-bye, pointing to objects, holding a hand out to receive an object from the person, and nodding or shaking the head. The person's response will indicate his or her understanding or lack of understanding of the gesture.

Simple Discrimination The above method can take quite some time to implement and may actually facilitate the individual's understanding as many of the objects and activities are in context (i.e., in familiar settings in which they would normally be found). Another way to determine a person's receptive language is to use a simple two choice discrimination task. It is generally faster than assessing during daily events and is useful for examining the person's receptive language without context cues. This is accomplished by presenting two objects to the person, naming them, and then asking him or her to pick up, look at, or point to a specific object. A form for collecting data for the discrimination task is shown in the Appendix (see

Appendix A.9). However, for some individuals, formal assessment settings are a stimulus for noncompliance and, thus, do not provide useful information on comprehension.

Association of Real Objects, Activities, and Locations to Referents In addition to assessment of basic language comprehension, it is also helpful to assess the person's ability to associate real objects, activities, or locations with symbols of the objects at varying levels of abstraction. One procedure is to show the person a real object and then have him or her choose between two line drawings, one of the object that is present and one of a different object. For example, a youngster is shown a real ball, and is then presented with two line drawings, one of a ball and one of a wagon. The child is then asked to find the picture of the ball. This method can be used with a variety of objects and activities, and with a variety of communication symbols. Figure 5.2 presents a hierarchy of symbols at various levels of abstraction that can be used for this assessment.

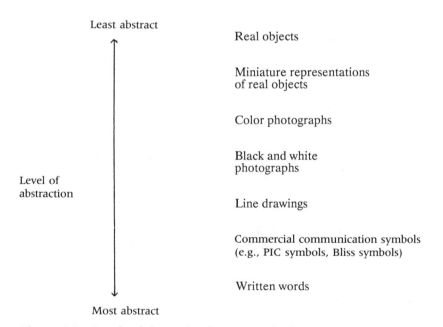

Figure 5.2. Levels of abstraction for communication systems.

Use of the Results The results of these assessments provide information critical for developing an effective communication system. Examine the list of receptive vocabulary obtained from the natural and structured observations. What words and/or phrases does the individual understand? In which settings and activities are they understood? Are gestural cues necessary for comprehension? Is the context necessary for comprehension? Are common gestures (e.g., waving, pointing) readily comprehended? Answer these questions, and then develop a priority list of vocabulary that is understood by the individual and a description of how to enhance his or her comprehension.

SUMMARY

Prior to designing a communication system for an individual with severe disabilities, the person's cognitive, motor, sensory, and speech and language abilities must be examined. Often, more formalized instruments do not provide information detailed enough to develop appropriate systems. The information most frequently missing is the person's ability to visually track and scan, his or her hand preference, and specific individualized information on basic receptive language skills, discrimination, and ability to associate real objects, activities, or events with abstract referents such as miniatures, line drawings, photographs, or parts of real objects. This chapter briefly discusses the need for assessing these abilities and suggests some methods for assessment. In addition, some suggestions for incorporating the results into the development of a communication system are provided.

ASSESSMENT RESOURCES

The following references are provided as a guide to some of the resources available on the assessment of students with moderate or severe handicaps. This list is not meant to be exhaustive but rather representative of some of the philosophy and techniques available to practitioners.

GENERAL ASSESSMENT

Bailey, D.B., Jr., & Wolery, M. (1989). *Assessing infants and pre-schoolers with handicaps*. Columbus, OH: Charles E. Merrill.

Browder, D.M. (1987). *Assessment of individuals with severe handicaps: An applied behavior approach to life skills assessment*. Baltimore: Paul H. Brookes Publishing Co.

Cohen, M.A., & Gross, P.J. (1979). *The developmental resource: Behavioral sequencing for assessment and program planning* (Vols. 1–2). New York: Grune & Stratton.

Peck, C.A., Schuler, A.L., Tomlinson, C., & Theimer, R.K. (no date). *Assessment handbook*. Santa Barbara, CA: Social Competence Curriculum Project, University of California.

BEHAVIORAL ASSESSMENT

Durand, V.M. (1986). *Motivation Assessment Scale*. Suffolk, NY: Suffolk Child Developmental Center.

Durand, V.M., & Crimmins, D.B. (1988). Identifying the variables maintaining self-injurious behavior. *Journal of Autism and Developmental Disorders, 18*(1), 99–117.

Evans, I.M., & Wilson, F.E. (1983). Behavioral assessment as decision making: A theoretical analysis. In M. Rosenbaum, C.M.

Franks, & Y. Jaffe (Eds.), *Perspectives on behavior therapy in the eighties* (pp. 35–53). New York: Springer-Verlag.

Freeman, B.J., Ritvo, E.R., Guthrie, D., Schroth, P., & Ball, J. (1978). The behavior observation scale for autism. *Journal of the American Academy of Child Psychiatry, 17,* 576–588.

Nihira, K., Foster, R., Shellhaas, M., & Leland, H. (1984). *AAMD Adaptive Behavior Scale* (rev. ed.). Washington, DC: American Association on Mental Deficiency.

Sailor, W., & Mix, B.J. (1975). *The TARC Assessment System.* Lawrence, KS: H & H Enterprises.

Sparrow, S.S., Balia, D.A., & Cicchetti, D.V. (1984). *Vineland Adaptive Behavior Scales.* Circle Pines, MN: American Guidance Service.

COGNITIVE ASSESSMENT

Arthur, G. (1950). *The Arthur Adaptation of the Leiter International Performance Scale.* Chicago: C.H. Stoelting.

Feuerstein, R. (1979). *The dynamic assessment of retarded performers.* Baltimore: University Park Press.

Haywood, H.C., Filler, J.W., Shifman, M.A., & Chatelanat, G. (1975). Behavioral assessment in mental retardation. In P. Reynolds (Ed.), *Advances in psychological assessment* (Vol. 3, pp. 27–55). San Francisco: Jossey-Bass.

Langley, M.B. (1989). Assessing infant cognitive development. In D.B. Bailey, Jr., & M. Wolery (Eds.), *Assessing infants and preschoolers with handicaps* (pp. 249–274). Columbus, OH: Charles E. Merrill.

Paget, K.D. (1989). Assessment of cognitive skills in the preschool-aged child. In D.B. Bailey, Jr., & M. Wolery (Eds.), *Assessing infants and preschoolers with handicaps* (pp. 275–300). Columbus, OH: Charles E. Merrill.

Stillman, R. (Ed.). (1978). *The Callier-Azusa Scale.* Dallas, TX: The University of Texas at Dallas, Callier Center for Communication Disorders.

FINE AND GROSS MOTOR ASSESSMENT

Bobath, B. (1978). *Adult hemiplegia: Evaluation and treatment* (2nd ed.). London: William Heinemann Medical Books.

Bobath, B., & Bobath, K. (1981). *Motor development in different types of cerebral palsy*. London: William Heinemann Medical Books.

Chandler, L. (1979). Gross and fine motor development. In M.A. Cohen & P.J. Gross, *The developmental resource: Behavioral sequencing for assessment and program planning* (Vol. 1, pp. 119–156). New York: Grune & Stratton.

Finnie, N.R. (1974). *Handling the young cerebral palsied child at home*. New York: E.P. Dutton.

Schurman, J.A. (1974). Custom designing communication board frames: The role of the occupational therapist. In B. Vicker (Ed.), *Nonoral communication system project* (pp. 179–211). Iowa City: Campus Stores Publishers.

Silverman, F.H. (1980). *Communication for the speechless*. Englewood Cliffs, NJ: Prentice-Hall.

Sternat, J., Nietupski, J., Lyon, S., Messina, R., & Brown, L. (1976). Integrated vs. isolated therapy models. In L. Brown, N. Scheuerman, & T. Crowner (Eds.), *Madison's alternative for zero exclusion: Toward an integrated therapy model for teaching motor, tracking and scanning skills to severely handicapped students* (pp. 1–9). Madison, WI: Madison Public Schools and University of Wisconsin-Madison.

Sternat, J., & Messina, R. (1976). Neurophysiological principles: Considerations for the development of educational curricula for severely handicapped students. In L. Brown, N. Scheuerman, & E.T. Crowner (Eds.), *Madison's alternative for zero exclusion: Toward an integrated therapy model for teaching motor, tracking and scanning skills to severely handicapped students* (pp. 10–15). Madison, WI: Madison Public Schools and University of Wisconsin-Madison.

PRAGMATICS ASSESSMENT

Donnellan, A.M., Mirenda, P., Mesaro, R.A., & Fassbender, L.L. (1984). Analyzing the communicative functions of aberrant behavior. *Journal of the Association for Persons with Severe Handicaps, 9,* 201–211.

Peck, C.A., & Schuler, A.L. (1987). Assessment of social/communicative behavior for students with autism and severe handicaps: The importance of asking the right question. In T.L. Layton (Ed.), *Lan-*

guage and treatment of autistic and developmentally disordered children (pp. 33–62). Springfield, IL: Charles C Thomas.

Schuler, A.L., & Goetz, L. (1981). The assessment of severe language disabilities: Communicative and cognitive considerations. *Analysis and Intervention in Developmental Disabilities, 1,* 333–346.

Wiig, E.H. (1982). *Let's talk inventory for adolescents.* Columbus, OH: Charles E. Merrill.

Wiig, E.H., & Bray, C.M. (1983). *Let's talk for children.* Columbus, OH: Charles E. Merrill.

INSTRUCTIONAL STRATEGIES

Falvey, M., Brown, L., Lyon, S., Baumgart, D., & Schroeder, J. (1980). Strategies for using cues and correction procedures. In W. Sailor, B. Wilcox, & L. Brown (Eds.), *Methods of instruction for severely handicapped students* (pp. 109–133). Baltimore: Paul H. Brookes Publishing Co.

Fey, M.E. (1986). *Language intervention with young children.* San Diego, CA: College-Hill Press.

Miller, J., & Allaire, J. (1987). Augmentative communication. In M.A. Snell (Ed.), *Systematic instruction of persons with severe handicaps,* (3rd ed., pp. 273–297). Columbus, OH: Charles E. Merrill.

Peck, C.A., & Schuler, A. (1983). *Instructional techniques for promoting social/communicative development.* Santa Barbara, CA: Social Competence Curriculum Project, University of California.

Pelland, M., & Falvey, M.A. (1986). Instructional strategies. In M.A. Falvey, *Community-based curriculum: Instructional strategies for students with severe handicaps.* Baltimore: Paul H. Brookes Publishing Co.

Siegel-Causey, E., & Downing, J. (1987). Nonsymbolic communication development: Theoretical concepts and educational strategies. In L. Goetz, D. Guess, & K. Stremel-Campbell (Eds.), *Innovative program design for individuals with dual sensory impairments* (pp.15–48). Baltimore: Paul H. Brookes Publishing Co.

Siegel-Causey, E., & Guess, D. (1989). *Enhancing nonsymbolic communication interactions among learners with severe disabilities.* Baltimore: Paul H. Brookes Publishing Co.

Snell, M.A., & Zirpoli, T.J. (1987). Intervention strategies. In M.A.

Snell (Ed.), *Systematic instruction of persons with severe handicaps* (pp.110–149). Columbus: Charles E. Merrill.

AUGMENTATIVE AND ALTERNATIVE SYSTEMS AND MATERIALS

Burkhart, L.J. (1980). *Homemade battery powered toys and education devices for severely handicapped children.* (Available from Linda J. Burkhart, R.D. 1, Box 124, Millville, PA 17846)

Burkhart, L.J. (1982). *More homemade battery devices for severely handicapped children with suggested activities.* (Available from Linda J. Burkhart, R.D.1, Box 124, Millville, PA 17846)

Hardy, G.M. (1980). *Nonoral communication project: A training guide for the child without speech.* (Available from the California Department of Education, P.O. Box 8510, Fountain Valley, CA 92708)

Fishman, I. (1987). *Electronic communication aids: Selection and use.* Boston: College-Hill Press.

Levin, J., & Scherfenberg, L. (1987). *Selection and use of simple technology in home, school, work, and community settings.* Minneapolis, MN: ABLENET.

Mayer-Johnson, R. (1988). *The picture communication symbols: Book I.* Solana Beach, CA: Mayer-Johnson Company.

Mayer-Johnson, R. (1988). *The picture communication symbols: Book II.* Solana Beach, CA: Mayer-Johnson Company.

McCormick, L., & Shane, H. (1984). Augmentative communication. In L.Mccormick & R.L. Schiefelbusch (Eds.), *Early language intervention: An introduction* (pp.325–356). Columbus, OH: Charles E. Merrill.

Musselwhite, C.R., & St. Louis, K.W. (1988). *Communication programming for persons with severe handicaps: Vocal and augmentative strategies.* San Diego: College-Hill Press.

Nietupski, J., & Hamre-Nietupski, S. (1977). Nonverbal communication and severely handicapped students: A review of selected literature. In L. Brown, J. Nietupski, S. Lyon, S. Hamre-Nietupski, T. Crowner, & L. Gruenewald (Eds.), *Curricular strategies for teaching functional object use, nonverbal communication, problem solving, and mealtime skills to severely handicapped students* (pp. 68–93). Madison, WI: Madison Public Schools and University of Wisconsin-Madison.

Schuler, A.L. (1983). *Selecting alternative communication systems for students with limited communication skills.* Santa Barbara, CA: Social Competence Curriculum Project, University of California.

Silverman, F.H. (1980). *Communication for the speechless.* Englewood Cliffs, NJ: Prentice-Hall.

Vanderheiden, G.C., & Grilley, K. (Eds.). (1976). *Nonvocal communication techniques and aids for the severely physically handicapped.* Baltimore: University Park Press.

Vicker, B. (Ed.). (1974). *Nonoral communication system project.* Iowa City: The University of Iowa.

CHAPTER
SIX

Factors Salient in Systems Used by Preschool Children

The case histories presented in this chapter involve preschool children with moderate to severe disabilites. In general, there are factors more salient for this age group that must be considered in the assessment and implementation of an augmentative or alternative communication system. All of the factors are related to the environments and contexts within which communication occurs. These five factors are presented below.

FACTOR 1: EMPHASIS ON SOCIO-COMMUNICATIVE SKILLS

At the preschool level, communication skills and social competence receive heavy emphasis (Filler, Baumgart, & Askvig,

1989). Most preschool activities require active interaction between adults and/or children on a constant level. As one
preschool teacher stated, "My whole program is communication!" (K. Stockbridge, personal communication, May 5,
1989).

For this reason, it is crucial that augmentative or alternative communication systems fit into these various communication contexts with ease. The system should be clear to and
usable with both adults and peers. It should reflect the types of
comments that a child might want to say in these daily activities. The system, its use, and instruction with it must be as
embedded within these daily activities as communication is for
children who have no difficulties learning language. A pull-out
model of communication therapy (where the child and therapist work together in a separate room) would not serve the
child well.

FACTOR 2: FAMILY/CAREGIVER INVOLVEMENT

When the typical daily schedules of preschool children are
examined, it becomes apparent that a large proportion of the
day is spent with caregivers. In addition, decisions about their
activities, clothes, toys, and playmates involve them, but are
heavily weighted by parental/guardian preferences. Thus, a
system should have significant input from the family/care-
givers and be useable in these settings. In the first case study of
Kevin, the parents and family are intimately involved in the
development and use of the communication system. In the
second case study of Ricky, the grandmother is the primary
caregiver and has developed a system of understanding Ricky's
signals that she prefers to use. Ricky's augmentative system
was developed to reflect the system she had established as well
as a slightly more complex set of signals. The grandmother's
involvement with this newer system is minimal at present;
however, the team of professionals at school is continuing to
make efforts to involve her.

FACTOR 3: PROGNOSIS
FOR FURTHER DEVELOPMENT

Professionals are cognizant that the prognosis for continuing change in the communication skills of preschoolers remains open. Parent and teacher expectations are not as set as with older individuals with moderate to severe disabilities, and this is appropriate. This leads to a contradictory situation: everyone is willing to try something new, but they don't want to "give up" on speech as the mode for communicating.

Several reviews of the literature are available that provide strong evidence and arguments for the use of augmentative communication systems, even when there is hope for the development of oral language (e.g., Silverman, 1989). If and when speech becomes a more efficient modality of communication for the child, the augmentative system will fade naturally from use and speech will take over as the primary means of interacting. The examples available from research and from practice provide meaningful support for the implementation of an augmentative system with young, nonverbal children.

FACTOR 4: USING AGE-APPROPRIATE
ROUTINES FOR DEVELOPING COMMUNICATION

Some of the routines in a preschooler's day are similar to those experienced by an older individual, whereas some are quite different. Grooming, eating, and greeting are three routines that occur fairly commonly for all of us. The difference is that for a preschooler, expectations for their participation has been decreased. Professionals and parents/caregivers may be inclined to provide more for the younger child without asking for his or her involvement. For example, a parent might comb the child's hair and brush his or her teeth without asking whether he or she would like to participate.

This often occurs whether or not the child has a disability. In these types of routines, all communication partners should be encouraged to allow the child to choose and perform some of the tasks without assistance.

Contradictorily, some routines are specific to young children. It would be embarassing to play "peek-a-boo" with a 15-year-old or an adult, but there is no hesitation when engaging in this routine with a 2-year-old. Songs, nursery rhymes, and made-up verbal games are common and, according to Bruner (1974/1975), are important to learning the roles and responsibilities that one has in communicative interactions. Augmentative or alternative communication systems for preschoolers with disabilites must be able to fit into the more typical routines of daily living as well as the routines that are characteristic of a child at 2, 3, 4, or 5 years of age.

FACTOR 5: USE OF SIMPLIFIED LANGUAGE

In the American culture, adults commonly simplify their language when speaking to young children (Snow, 1972). McDonald (1985) and Tingey (1989) review research that has shown that the use of simplified language facilitates the learning of language by children who are having difficulties. When working with preschoolers on augmentative communication, professionals and parents/caregivers should take advantage of these tendencies and highlight them in interactions. All communication partners should be encouraged to keep their language simple and to use the communication system in a simple manner that follows their verbal utterances. Instead of just saying, "You want more milk in your blue cup?," the partner could say, "Milk? Cup? Milk in cup?" while pointing to the pictures of milk and cup, or could emphasize with integration key words while using typical sentence structures, such as, "You want more *milk* in your *cup*."

The case histories presented here provide two examples of how these factors were considered in the implementation of systems for communicating. Furthermore, each child has specific needs and abilities for which the system was designed. As detailed in previous chapters, the emphasis in both cases was on identifing existing signals as meaningful forms of communication. Their use was then restructured in daily activities to enhance understanding by the child and his or her communication partners.

KEVIN

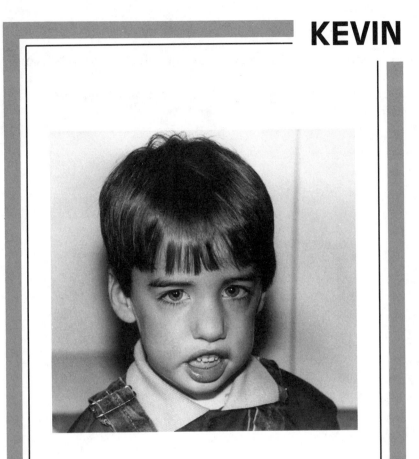

NAME: Kevin
AGE: 3 years, 6
                 months
TEACHER: Kathy
CONSULTANT: J. Johnson

SYSTEM

An object system followed by a picture system were designed and used successfully by Kevin. The second system consisted of colored catalogue pictures mounted on index cards and were filed and stored in a shoe box.

OVERVIEW

Kevin's teacher, Kathy, contacted the consultant because she and Kevin's parents were concerned about furthering his communication skills. Kathy had conducted a nonstandardized assessment of Kevin's communication and was considering changing his current signing program. Kevin had been taught signing, but little progress had been made. His signing was limited in vocabulary and was not used spontaneously after many months of intervention. His speech was limited to vowel-like vocalizations and he did not imitate novel sounds. Kevin's parents wondered if a communication book would be appropriate since Kevin was interested in pictures. They recognized many different types of idiosyncratic communicative signals already used by Kevin and tried to respond to the signals in a meaningful manner. However, all of the communication partners, including Kevin, expressed frustration when using this system.

Kevin was diagnosed at birth as having myotonic dystrophy, a rare, slowly progressive, hereditary disease characterized by muscular atrophy of the face and neck muscles (*Dorland's Illustrated Medical Dictionary*, 1981). His facial expressions are quite subtle. According to his mother, enjoyment is expressed through a slight raising of the lower eyelids, increased body movement, and vocalization. These signals are difficult for unfamiliar communication partners to interpret.

Kevin was referred for special services immediately after he was born. He was delayed in the areas of motor skills, cognition, and communication. At the beginning of the current school year, it was noted that self-help, cognitive, social, and communication skills range between 12–24 months according to nonstandardized, criterion-referenced testing. As for motor skills, Kevin has been walking for about one year. He shows a preference for manipulating small items such as beads and paper clips. Vision and hearing are thought to be normal.

Kevin first received special education services through a private, nonprofit center for infants and toddlers with disabilities. His program concentrated on enhancing motor skills, cognitive skills such as object exploration, and developing vocal and nonvocal communication.

Kevin entered the public school system at the age of 3. He has attended a half-day preschool program for toddlers who are handicapped since that time. He has received speech therapy once a week with the school communication disorders specialist (CDS). Additionally, Kevin has been receiving speech and language therapy through a nearby university communication disorders clinic.

The emphasis for Kevin in the educational setting has been to increase independence in self-help skills, to encourage fine and gross motor exploration of the environment, to improve social interaction skills with peers and adults, and to enhance communication skills. The focus in speech therapy provided by the schools has been to encourage signing and differentiated vocalizations. The university clinic has also focused on signing in order to provide support for the school program.

At home, Kevin used the sign "MILK" to request milk. He would also bring a desired object or food to his parents or pull his parents to the refrigerator and touch what he wanted. If a picture was informally available, his parents noted that, on occasion, he would touch the picture of the item he wanted. When frustrated during these attempts to communicate, he was reported to vocalize (e.g., "eeeee") and run away, flapping his hands in front of his chest. If asked to stay seated, he complied.

ASSESSMENT

A standardized assessment of cognitive and communication skills had not been completed as of the time of the consultation, according to public school records, due to difficulties in getting Kevin to perform the tasks that are required. The school intervention team decided to use the preschool teacher's nonstandardized assessment results from the beginning of the 1988–1989 school year for determining program objectives. Much of the information from this assessment was used by the consultant, J. Johnson, in suggesting changes for Kevin's communication system.

The nonstandardized assessment that was used with Kevin examined sensorimotor skills and communicative forms and functions through a technique recommended by Stonestreet, Augustine, and Johnson (1986). This technique is based on the transactional model of language (Bloom & Lahey, 1978; McLean & Snyder-McLean, 1978) in which the content, form, and use of prelinguistic communication are considered integral components of development. By setting up what Wetherby and Prizant (1989) termed "communication temptations," information about each of these areas was obtained. The teacher observed or created opportunities for such behaviors to occur in naturalistic settings so that generalizations could be made about Kevin's skills.

The consultant observed in the classroom during the second half of the 1988–1989 school year. Kathy had continued to update her assessment information to that date. The consultant collected data from Kathy's files on Kevin, interviewed the parents and classroom aides, performed direct observations, and elicited particular behaviors from Kevin. The cumulative efforts are reported in the following section.

Content

The data on Content were compiled from all of the sources that were previously mentioned.

1. Object skills—Kevin used objects and toys conventionally. For example, he drew with a pencil, brought a toothbrush to his mouth, put a toy phone to his ear and said, "Dada" (and sometimes put the receiver in his mouth), and put the comb to his own hair. He explored unique properties of novel objects, inspecting and manipulating the parts. In a play setting, Kevin sorted objects into like categories based on shape; however, in formal tasks of matching pictures to objects, Kevin's responses were variable. This indicated that Kevin knew how common objects are used, understood that toys are representations of the actual object, and saw similarities among objects. Further assessment was necessary to ascertain his ability to recognize pictures as representations of objects. This was accomplished by asking Kevin's parents whether or not Kevin seemed to be interested in pictures and what he did with the pictures. His mother reported that he liked to look through magazines and had once indicated he wanted "milk" by using a picture. No other evidence was found using direct or retrospective observations.

2. Means-ends skills—This was an interesting area to assess because Kevin did not persist in motor activities that were difficult or that required strength. This may have been related to his diagnosed condition. Nevertheless, Kevin was observed turning a knob on a play radio, listening to the music, and then moving on to another activity. Given a lidded plastic jar containing a cookie, Kevin picked up the jar, examined it, and put it down to go on to another activity. When the lid was left loosely threaded, Kevin removed it to get the cookie. As mentioned, he used adults as vehicles to reach his goal by, for example, pulling them to the refrigerator to get food and sometimes using a picture to indicate his desires. He also used a knife and a cookie cutter to press on play-doh, stopping to examine the effect of his efforts. These combined activities indicated that Kevin could use social and nonsocial intermediary means to reach his goal.

3. Object permanence skills—Although the literature on the

relation of object permanence to language development is inconclusive (Rice, 1984), the ability to hold the image of an object in mind when it is not present seems to be a logical underpinning to the ability to use representations to indicate a nonpresent object. Without trying to make a case for or against this hypothesis, the data were collected and presented as follows.

Once again, it was difficult to assess Kevin's abilities. When a desired object was partially hidden in several trials, Kevin consistently retrieved it. When the same object was entirely covered, Kevin sometimes looked at the place it disappeared, sometimes lifted the blanket, but always left to go on to another activity. The assessment team hypothesized either that Kevin may have been interpreting the assessment team's behaviors as signals to terminate joint attention to that object, or that his skills in object permanence were still developing.

In summary, it appeared that many of Kevin's behaviors were typical of those seen in Piaget's Sensorimotor Stage IV and V, with some skills, such as tool use, indicating higher levels of knowledge. It was more important for the purpose of programming, however, to examine the implications of the behaviors rather than to assign a "level." From the assessment, it appeared that Kevin was ready for a communication system that had a rudimentary symbolic component to it. He used toys as real objects indicating an ability to symbolize given an icon or a highly similar representation. It was not clear, however, how well Kevin understood that pictures stood for the object they represented.

Form and Use

The form and use data are taken from all of the available aforementioned sources. Data collected using the Form and Use Assessment Sheet (see Appendix A.7) is shown in Figure 6.1.

1. Receptive form and use skills—Receptive skills refer to Kevin's ability to understand the communication signals of

Form and Use Assessment Sheet

Name of client: _Kevin_

Observer: _Johnson_   Date: _April, 1989_

Context	Partner	Child signal	Partner response	Discourse function	Pragmatic function
Play time cue: "Ok, go get the monkeys, Kevin."	Kathy	Looks at Kathy	Looks back, eyebrows raised, "Monkeys, Kevin," points	Maintain	Request for clarification
		Goes to shelf and takes out monkeys	"Un-huh"	Maintain	Acknowledgment
Small Group: Sitting at table with two peers and two adults, playing with play-doh	Aide	"Eeee," looks at aide, holds up play-doh	"Ooooh—a pancake"	Initiate	Comment or show-off
Aide makes snake with play-doh and holds it up for Kevin, "See?"	Aide	"Eeee," lower eyelids raised	"A snake"	Maintain	Acknowledgment
		"Eeee," gives Aide his play-doh	"What, you want a snake?," makes snake	Initiate	Request for action
	Peer	Reaches for cookie cutter	"It's mine," pulls it away	Initiate	Request for object
	Peer	"Eeee!," runs away, hands flapping	"You can't have it!"	Terminate or maintain	Protest
Tickle routine cue: "Tickle, tickle, tickle . . ."	Kathy	Lifts up shirt to expose tummy	"More? Ok, tickle, tickle . . ."	Maintain	Request for social routine

Figure 6.1. Sample of form and use data for Kevin. (Discourse functions served by the child's signal: initiate, maintain, terminate, or repair conversation; pragmatic functions of the child's signal: request object or action, protest, request social routine, greeting, showing off, calling, request permission, acknowledgment, comment, request information, clarification [see Wetherby and Prizant, 1989 or Chapter Two for definitions]).

others. During playtime, Kevin pointed to the doll's eyes when asked, "Where are eyes?" and retrieved the correct toy from the shelf given a one-word verbal cue, "pegs," plus a point gesture. When communication partners used more than one-word utterances, or did not gesture, Kevin did not respond correctly to the request. If he was asked to retrieve a familiar object during activity transitions or during an activity other than playtime, Kevin did not respond. It appeared that Kevin understood single words in familiar routines within typical settings.

2. Expressive form and use skills—Expressive skills refer to Kevin's ability to produce communicative signals. As noted in Table 6.1, Kevin used the vocalization, "Eeee," with fluctuating pitch and loudness to express enjoyment and protest. His communication partners interpreted these signals as requests to continue or cease an activity. It was not always clear whether the communication partners had interpreted this signal correctly. He also said, "Dada," and held up his arms to be lifted. Once, when his mother moved in the room, the consultant heard him say, "Nana," as if it were a comment on her presence.

Kevin touched or reached for desired objects, often adding alternating gaze between the object and an adult. These signals were interpreted by all partners as requests for the object or requests for the name of the object. Facial expressions proved difficult to identify. Unfamiliar and familiar partners may have been influenced by his lax expression, often expressing the belief that Kevin was not interested in the activity.

3. Social interactions—There was no doubt that Kevin was intentionally attempting to interact with peers and adults by using vocalizations and gestures. When the teacher initiated a tickle routine and then paused, Kevin lifted up his shirt to request continuation of the routine. If an adult imitated his sounds, Kevin made the sound again and looked at the adult.

Kevin's active participation in social interactions was supported by his ability to anticipate portions of classroom routines. In morning circle, for example, he filled in the hand motions for a favorite song when the teacher paused midsong and looked expectantly at Kevin. His responsiveness also encouraged others to interact with him. For instance, when Kevin's parents entered the room, he ran over to them vocalizing, "Eeee," as a greeting not easily ignored.

In summary, Kevin participated in the social frame of communication as an initiator and responder when given the opportunity to do so. He had limited vocalizations and verbalizations and yet accomplished communicative goals through gestural means with some success. With these limited forms, he had developed a wide repertoire of communicative functions. Kevin intentionally used communicative means to regulate the behavior of others, to establish and maintain social interaction, and to establish or maintain joint attention to an object or event (Wetherby & Prizant, 1989). His partners, however, often had difficulty interpreting his facial expressions and other signals and had attributed a "lack of interest" in activities to his limited facial expressions.

ASSESSMENT FOR COMMUNICATION SYSTEM PLANNING

Question 1:   What Type of Symbols Should Be Used in the System and How Should They Be Presented?

It was not clear from assessment and anecdotal data whether Kevin clearly understood that pictures represent objects. Instead of waiting to assess further, it was decided to implement an intermediary system that met current needs and skills while assessing object-to-picture matching skills. The intermediary system consisted of two to three object choices placed on the table at snacktime and playtime at home and at school. For example, during snacktime, a cup just like his assigned cup was laid on the table to represent "drink" and an empty cracker box was presented to represent "crackers." Kevin touched what he wanted and was presented with a matching object or food item. Since Kevin was already touching and getting the actual desired item, it was felt that this next level of representation would not be too difficult.

Kevin needed no training with the intermediary system. Upon presentation of the object or food choice representations, he differentially touched his preferred choices. The idea that the items touched were not the ones received did not seem to cause hesitation on Kevin's part. Given choices of less desired food or toys, Kevin consistently touched his favorite items regardless of how they were arranged on the table. If the adult responded incorrectly, Kevin ignored the offered item and again touched his preferred choice. This system was implemented at school, at home, and at the university clinic by the teacher, aides, parents, and student clinician. Specific data for Kevin's behavior were not kept because he was so accurate in his responses at the outset. Data was collected for use of the system by the aides who had the most trouble interpreting his signals. The data indicated an increase of 57% (a change from 30% to 87%) in the number of responses to Kevin's signals over a 3-month period.

Question 2:   Does Kevin Understand Pictures as Representations of Objects?

The original plan in assessing object-to-picture matching was to: 1) introduce pictures near the objects during actual choice-making situations, and 2) match pictures to objects during a play situation. Kevin quickly showed his partners that he was ready for the use of pictures without the support of matching objects. At school, Kevin's teacher cut out catalogue pictures of the toys available for free time and laminated them individually on 3 inch by 5 inch cards. Before she could arrange the pictures of the three possible activities on the table in front of Kevin, he took the picture of his favorite toy and gave it to Kathy. She responded by immediately allowing Kevin to go play with that toy. A similar incident occurred in the university clinic. The student clinician was arranging the objects and pictures on the table for snacktime when Kevin reached over the objects and took the picture of his favorite cookie. The clinician responded by giving him one of those cookies. Kevin's parents, his teacher, classroom aides, and the student clinician decided to forego the objects and use colored pictures when possible in these choice-making situations. They also decided to provide a varying number of choices depending on the context and what they wanted to make available. An example of Kevin using the object system is shown in Figure 6.2.

To make sure Kevin was truly choosing differentially, pictures of less preferred items were presented with two preferred items. Once again, regardless of the position of the pictures, Kevin touched only his favorite items. If the adult responded incorrectly, Kevin vocalized, "Eeee," and ran away to express protest and frustration. After a pause by the adult, Kevin would return and touch the preferred item again. Since he was ini-

Figure 6.2. Example of Kevin using an object system.

tially so accurate on this system, no data were collected regarding knowledge of the relationship between the object and its picture. Figure 6.3 shows the teacher giving Kevin the picture he had chosen after such a sequence. Following this, Kevin took the picture to the shelf where the blocks in the picture were kept and began to play with them.

As can be seen, a nontraditional format was used for presenting pictures. Kevin is ambulatory and quite active, therefore, a single stationary communication board would not be efficient. Furthermore, the speed with which Kevin is progressing in the use of his communication system makes it difficult to design a particular style at this time. The teacher and Kevin's parents have expressed the preference for keeping shoe box files of individual picture choices, sorted according to activity, near the area where they are likely to be needed. Although the file at school is almost full, the emphasis continues to be on making or finding enough pictures to represent the items that

Figure 6.3. Example of Kevin using a picture system.

Kevin might want to select. Kevin enjoys looking through a 3–4 inch stack of pictures to make his selection, and he sometimes does it just for enjoyment.

Currently, Kevin's student clinician and teacher are experimenting with more abstract representations of choices. To date, Kevin has been 30% accurate in matching black line drawings on a white background to the objects they represent or to the colored catalogue pictures he is currently using. It would appear that the colored pictures are the most efficient communication form for Kevin at this time.

Question 3: What Are Kevin's Vocabulary Needs in Everyday Interactions? Which Words Would Be Most Powerful with Partners?

Potential vocabulary items were gathered by Kevin's most frequent adult communication partners. Each adult made a schedule of their typical day with him. Within these schedules, repetitive events, such as play and snack, occurred frequently with various partners. Each partner agreed to give Kevin at least one opportunity to make a choice during these play and snack activities. The partners were encouraged to select choices that they felt Kevin would want to make and for which they did not mind giving up control. After this general description by the consultant and the admonition to "Stay simple," Kevin's teacher and parents began to make the picture vocabulary and present the choices. As mentioned, the number of vocabulary pictures has now soared, barely keeping up with Kevin's abilities. Additionally, recent reports from both parties indicate that Kevin is offered choices throughout the day, limited only by the time-consuming job of finding enough pictures. If Kevin wants something other than what is pictured, he resorts to his old system of touching the desired item when possible.

The one vocabulary item, felt by many partners to be a necessity, was a more acceptable representation for "no." As mentioned, Kevin would run away to protest or reject an object. It was decided that the partners would respond to Kevin when he turned away while still in his chair. This behavior was observed to precede the running away. The partners agreed to say, "No? OK," in situations where other choices were available. The implementation of this system occurred near the end of the 1988–1989 school year, so the results are unclear as yet. It is hoped, however, that this signal can be further shaped into pushing the object away.

Since Kevin's vocabulary is so diverse, the issue of selecting "the most powerful" words is moot. All of the cards serve as significant means of communicating with others. Kevin's classmates have begun to use the system spontaneously, often imitating the exact intonations of the aides and the teacher, particularly during play. The consultant observed two incidents where the pictures were used by peers as a negotiating mechanism to trade toys.

One sign that his needs are more adequately met with this system is the notable reduction in his expressions of frustration. As mentioned, when an adult responded incorrectly, Kevin would run off, flapping his hands. His parents and teacher have remarked that he will persist in selecting choices for a longer period, showing frustration only when he is prevented from obtaining a chosen item. This change is gratifying because now his frustration is related to the outcome of communicating rather than to the process of trying to communicate. That is, his partners understand clearly what he wants even though he cannot always have his choice. Prior to this, his partners were struggling merely to understand his signals.

Question 4: Can the System Be Integrated into Numerous Social Interactions? Can All Communication Partners Be Trained to Use the System?

Kevin had extremely cooperative communication partners both at home, at school, and at the university clinic. This enabled swift integration of the communication system into many settings simultaneously. Moreover, the system lent itself easily to translation by more than one partner. After only a brief description of how Kevin is allowed to make a choice, new partners, such as the speech and language pathologist and other family members, have used the system and interpreted initiations and responses quite accurately. The only aspect that requires continued monitoring by the teacher is ensuring that these new partners provide ample opportunities for choice-making.

In retrospect, this seems like a "pollyanna" case—eager teacher, eager parents, the child's ease in learning the system, follow through on building and using the system—all of the perfect ingredients that are sought when setting out to implement an augmentative communication system. In reality, this case history is a good example of how the weight of the success of appropriate intervention often falls on the shoulders of those who surround the child rather than on the child's "motivation."

It is likely that Kevin is motivated because he has a system that matches his current skills and gives him power to manipulate others. He could easily have become bored if the pictures had remained limited in their scope, were too abstract in representation, or had not represented his preferences. This may be why the signing system was not used as it was hoped; sign language is a highly abstract means of representation. Kevin's sensorimotor abilities suggested that an iconic symbol system was more appropriate. Similarly, Kevin may have appeared unmotivated if his partners had only used the pictures during controlled, instructional table tasks (i.e., Adult initiates, "What's this, Kevin?" Adult holds up object. Kevin points to picture. Adult responds, "Good job!"). Because his partners allowed him to use the pictures in naturally occurring routines to make significant, meaningful requests (from Kevin's perspective), he quickly learned and seemed to enjoy this new way of exerting control.

Question 5: What Next?

To maintain this level of motivation, it is crucial to remain flexible in expanding Kevin's system. First, the prognosis for oral language is not clear. Kevin's mother, who also has this syndrome, has normal speech and language. The added component of mental retardation in Kevin's case makes a prognosis for speech and language difficult. Since Kevin is so young, the effort to expand vocalizations and verbalizations should continue in earnest in combination with the picture system. For example, if Kevin vocalizes while using the pictures, the adult can interpret the vocalization as if it was related to the picture (e.g., Kevin, "Eeee." Adult, "Yes, pegs."). If oral communication becomes more functional and efficient for Kevin, experience indicates that the augmentative system will likely fade from use. It is also for this reason that an electronic device with synthesized speech was not chosen. Synthesized speech interrupts a person's efforts to vocalize or verbalize since the two often occur simultaneously.

Second, efforts to ensure that his communication system reflects current needs must continue. New vocabulary for new partners and routines should be added as needed in the established format. For example, if Kevin is mainstreamed into a regular classroom for art, some pictures relating to choices for that day's art project would be appropriate. At the same time, the educational team will teach Kevin to use more abstract line drawings to gradually replace the catalogue pictures. Line drawings are available commercially and are easier to reduce in size, creating the opportunity for communication books that have the pictures organized by "situation pages." This would be a faster system of presentation than leafing through files of pictures.

As Kevin gets older, words could be printed on all of the pictures or drawings to encourage sight-word vocabulary. Some of the pictures already have words printed on them; however, this is more for the partners than for Kevin. Written words would be a more efficient means of communication should speech remain nonfunctional and would provide an easy vehicle to using computers for academics, if they have not already been introduced.

SUMMARY

In summary, a picture communication system was designed for Kevin that was based on his ability to use pictures as symbolic representations of real objects as well as on his previously demonstrated preferences in daily routines. Kevin's ability to be understood increased in direct relation to the improvement in the ability of Kevin's partners to identify and interpret his signals.

RICKY

NAME: Ricky
AGE: 5 years, 7 months
TEACHER: Kathy
CONSULTANT: J. Johnson

SYSTEM

A system using real objects and food was used to specify choices during snacktime and mealtime. Additionally, adults provided more opportunities for expressing preferences in the context of other familiar activities.

OVERVIEW

Ricky was referred for consultation by his preschool teacher, Kathy. She had completed a nonstandardized assessment of socio-communicative skills, which is discussed below, and had requested ideas for programming related to her findings. Ricky did not have a communication system that was recognized by more than one partner. Some of Ricky's partners felt that he was apathetic about interacting because he did not look directly at them. Kathy wished to become more systematic in responding to Ricky's nonverbal signals.

The etiology of Ricky's condition is unknown. According to medical records, he has brain damage and grand mal seizures that are controlled with medication. His educational category is that of developmental delay. Self-help, cognitive, social, and communication skills currently range between 9 and 18 months based on criterion-referenced checklists. Ricky is ambulatory with adequate fine and gross motor skills. He is nonverbal and vocalizes infrequently. He lives with his grandmother and his father.

Ricky was first seen for assessment and special programming when he was 2 years old. Services were provided by a private nonprofit organization serving infants and toddlers with disabilities. At that time, delays in all areas of development, except gross motor skills, were noted.

122

Ricky entered the public school system at 3 years of age. The adjustments of seizure medication led to behaviors that consumed much of the intervention team's efforts during his first year in the program. Specifically, Ricky would force his whole hand in his mouth, gag, and vomit frequently throughout the day even though he was taking medication to control nausea. As one might guess, the process of prevention and clean-up was quite time consuming. During his second year in public school, the medication was changed and this behavior disappeared. At the time of this assessment, Kathy reported that Ricky had resumed the gagging behavior without the vomiting. She felt he used this behavior as a protest when he was prevented from having a desired item.

Educational programming in the public school was focused on improving social skills with peers and adults. Retrospective observations revealed that Ricky did not seek interaction with peers or adults in close proximity, yet he observed other's actions when he was at a distance. He did not make eye contact when he was near his communication partner, actively averting gaze when the partner persisted in trying to get his visual attention. As mentioned, this was interpreted as apathy or rejection by his partners. Unfortunately, a crucial factor regarding cultural gaze patterns appropriate to Ricky's Native American background had been overlooked, but this was not discovered until a program had been implemented to ameliorate the gaze aversion.

Ricky's grandmother confirmed the observations regarding interaction patterns. She told the teacher that Ricky picked up toys that had just been abandoned by his cousins and imitated their actions with the toys. When the cousins returned, Ricky moved away and watched. This report made the teacher believe that Ricky might not be apathetic about interactions after all.

Ricky's program also focused on self-help, cognitive, fine motor, and communication skills. He ate with his fingers and drank from a cup, but when he was finished, he would set the cup down without looking, often spilling the liquid. Ricky did not explore objects that were placed in front of him except to put them in his mouth. This required that an adult be nearby whenever he was given objects. He did not play with small items, but did enjoy spilling pegs and blocks out of containers around the room.

Communication with Ricky was difficult according to his teacher. Most of his partners were able to interpret the gag and lying on the floor with eyes closed as a protest, and reaching for an item as a request; however, since many of the objects that Ricky wanted were potentially dangerous, he was often prevented from having them. Maintaining a positive attitude toward Ricky was difficult for some. Many of his communication partners expressed frustration.

ASSESSMENT

The assessment followed the same nonstandardized technique as was used for Kevin, the first case history in this chapter. Ricky's understanding of verbal messages and the content of his own messages was examined by eliciting responses to Piagetian tasks and observing the contexts in which the messages were expressed. At the same time, the forms of existing signals were identified in conjunction with the functions that they served in particular situations. The assessment data are from the teacher's files and observations made by the consultant after the assessment had been completed.

Content

Many behaviors similar to those seen in Piaget's Sensorimotor Stages III and IV were noted. A description of the skills in the sensorimotor domains pertinent to the development of language (McLean & Snyder-McLean, 1978; Rice, 1984) follows:

1. Object relations—Ricky would briefly manipulate, mouth, and then drop objects without examining them visually. When prevented from putting objects in his mouth, he would manipulate the item a bit longer before dropping it. He showed differentiated actions only for food-related

items such as a toy bottle and a cup. The mouthing pattern for these objects was specific to their shape and to the process of obtaining food from them. For example, Ricky anticipated the nipple shape of the toy bottle by puckering his lips prior to sucking on the bottle; whereas, with the cup, he raised his lower lip and put his tongue forward. This was different from the mouthing pattern for other items.

Ricky noted similarities among some objects. He used all types of cups for drinking, treated all sizes of spoons as one, and, as mentioned, used the toy bottle as if it were a real bottle. This indicates some flexibility in his categories for familiar food-related objects. He did not respond to pictures as representations of objects and often mouthed them.

2. Means-ends skills—Ricky was observed to used direct means to achieve nonsocial goals. When given a pressure switch attached to a tape recorder, he attended to the movement of the switch rather than to the effect it created. When presented with a string attached quite obviously to a toy for which he had just reached, Ricky played with the string. These findings indicated that Ricky's communication system must provide immediate results related directly to the vocabulary display.

3. Object permanence—When an object of interest was suddenly completely covered, Ricky would pull the cover off. This indicated at least a short-term ability to hold an image of the object in his mind.

4. Imitation—Ricky imitated the actions of others when the movements were similar, but not exactly, the same as those he had already performed. If the action was entirely novel, he did not respond. This was an important indicator of his ability to attend to other individuals in the environment and his flexibility in motor schemes.

Conclusions The data on Content were interpreted in terms of the implications for augmenting communication. It seemed that Ricky was able to note similarities among some objects, to employ direct means to achieve goals, and to hold an image in mind for a brief period when the referent was suddenly completely covered. He did not recognize pictures as representations of objects. These factors indicated a need for an object-based communication system.

Forms and Use

The elicitation techniques summarized by Wetherby and Prizant (1989) and observation methods discussed in Chapter Three produced a clearer understanding of Ricky's lack of response to directions. Furthermore, a more complex set of forms and functions became evident than had been expected by those who knew Ricky well.

1. Receptive language—Ricky's teacher and the consultant were not convinced that Ricky was responding to the spoken language that was directed to him. Systematic variations of verbal cues with and without supporting gestures were presented during familiar activities throughout a 2-week period.

    Given only verbal one-word utterances, such as "no," "up," and "drink," without gestures or object cues, Ricky did not respond. When gestures were added or when the object was present, Ricky responded appropriately. For example, when Ricky was about to tip over a bin of pegs, and the aide said, "No," Ricky persisted. When the aide blocked Ricky's arm so he could not touch the bin, he made a "raspberry" (i.e., protruded tongue through lips while blowing) sound. Although this lack of response to prohibitive words is not unusual behavior for a preschooler, it occurred consistently with other familiar words as well. When the teacher said, "Drink?" without a cup present, Ricky did not pause or respond. When she brought out a cup with water, Ricky immediately took the cup and gulped the contents.

2. Expressive skills—The Form and Use Assessment Sheet (see Appendix A.7 for a blank form) was used to collect

information on forms and functions of communication. A sample of the data recorded is depicted in Figure 6.4.

As can be seen, the forms that Ricky uses for the function of requesting included reaching for items, taking adults to the desired item, and clapping his hands when an item was withheld. Ricky persisted in these behaviors during snack, for instance, until he had consumed several crackers and a cup of water. He showed protest or rejection by lying down on the floor with his eyes closed, pushing objects away, and/or emitting a raspberry sound. Ricky's grandmother noted that these were the signals Ricky used at home as well. Kathy remembered that Ricky also put his whole hand in his mouth and gagged when he had been prevented from engaging in an activity. Not all of Ricky's communication partners interpreted these signals in these ways, however. As a result, there was marked inconsistency in adult and peer responses to Ricky's communicative attempts.

Using Wetherby and Prizant's (1989) format for examining communicative intents (see Chapters Two and Three), it became clear that most of Ricky's forms were used for behavioral regulation. He had one form purely for social interaction that consisted of vocalizing and looking briefly at others at a distance. He did not use his signals for maintaining shared attention, as Wetherby and Prizant (1989) define it.

3. Intentionality and social interaction—It was clear that Ricky was intentionally trying to manipulate others through his communication signals and that many of his signals were successful in bringing about the desired result.

Social interactions were frequently interspersed with gaze aversion episodes when Ricky was in close proximity to others. This caused his partners to persist longer and move in closer in an attempt to gain visual attention. When the partner finally leaned back, Ricky was observed to glance briefly at the individual. At the time of initial assessment, the reason for this behavior was not clear and was thought to be an idiosyncrasy.

Form and Use Assessment Sheet

Name of client: Ricky Johnson

Observer: _____   Date: April, 1989

Context	Partner	Child signal	Partner response	Discourse function	Pragmatic function
Snack time: cookie and drink on tray	Kathy	Reaches for cookie	"Cookie? Ok."	Initiate	Request for food
Kathy reaches in bag for another cookie		Reaches toward Kathy, claps	"More? More cookie?"	Maintain	Request for food
Kathy gives Ricky cup instead of cookie		Pushes cup away, reach for cookie	"No drink. Ok."	Maintain	Protest and request
Playtime:	Aide	Takes Aide's hand and goes to sink	"What? You want a drink?"	Initiate	Request for drink
"No, no drink now . . ."		Raspberry	"Well!"	Maintain	Acknowledgment and/or protest
"No, you can't have a drink."		Lies down on floor and closes eyes	Ignores	Terminate	Protest
Playtime:	Peers	Looks at peers across room and vocalizes, "Uuuhhh"	None	Attempt to initiate	Calling

Figure 6.4. Sample of form and use data for Ricky. (Discourse functions served by the child's signal: initiate, maintain, terminate, or repair conversation; pragmatic functions of the child's signal: request object or action, protest, request social routine, greeting, showing off, calling, request permission, acknowledgment, comment, request information, clarification [see Wetherby and Prizant, 1989 or Chapter Two for definitions]).

ASSESSMENT OF
COMMUNICATION SYSTEM PLANNING

Six questions were asked regarding Ricky's abilities as they pertained to a communication system. The questions and discussion are presented below.

Question 1: Which Symbolic Forms Should Be Used for Ricky's Communication System?

It was decided that real objects, a symbolic form that Ricky already understood, should be used in structured choice-making situations such as snacktime. Since Ricky did not recognize pictures as representations, they were not considered as a possible symbolic form for his communication system. Figure 6.5 shows the teacher using the system by providing a food and a drink choice during snacktime.

Question 2: What Behaviors Should Be Used with These Symbolic Forms and What Functions Should They Serve?

The teacher and aides agreed to let Ricky have objects he touched, provided they were not dangerous. In other words, reaching for an object, as shown in Figure 6.5, constituted a signal for requesting. Pushing an object away, another existing signal, would be interpreted as a rejection of that item. Vocalizations from a distance were accepted as bids for attention during playtime and at recess. The context for responding to this last signal was specified so that Ricky could learn to assign meaning to this random and infrequent signal. When he vocalized, the adult who was nearest would walk toward him saying, "Yes?"

It was hoped that more conventional and polite forms could be substituted for rejection. Since Ricky already pushed items away, a gesture might be shaped where the palm of the hand was extended toward his partner to say, "Stop." The first

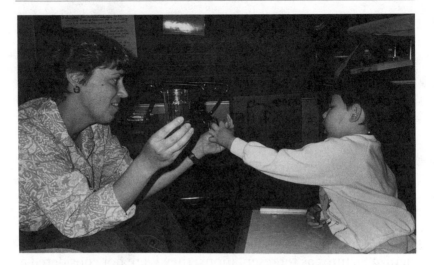

Figure 6.5. Example of Ricky using his real object system.

school year ended, however, before this effort could be initiated.

To summarize, the symbolic forms, behavioral forms, and functions for Ricky's communication system emerged from existing skills. The forms were identified and assigned communicative value by school personnel in specific situations. The focus in establishing this system was to unify the responses of communication partners rather than to change or fade to other forms of signals.

Question 3: What Format Should Be Used for Presenting Choices?

A two-item choice format was used. In structured situations, the choices were placed in front of Ricky to the right and left. Presenting more than two choices resulted in unclear signals. For instance, given a cup of water, cookie, and cracker, Ricky would move his hand from one item to the next without pausing. If only two items were presented, he reached for only one item. This pattern was evident regardless of the positioning of the items.

In unstructured situations, such as playtime in class, the teacher and aides agreed that, as in the past, one adult would follow Ricky as he walked around the room. When he paused near a toy shelf, the adult provided two choices of allowable toys, one to his right and one to his left. This provided Ricky more opportunities for choosing than he had previously been given.

The script for choice-making was nearly the same each time. The partner would say, "Drink?" and hold up the cup with water, and, "Cookie?" and hold up the cookie in the other hand. When Ricky reached for one item, it was given to him while the adult said the name of the item (e.g., "Cookie") with falling intonation. The position of the choices was randomly presented to verify the preference and to ensure that Ricky's choices were not based solely on location. Sometimes the communication partner would move the choices and ask a second time before Ricky's signal was acknowledged. In these instances, Ricky persisted in touching the same item regardless of its position. If the partner continued to withhold the food, Ricky would drop his hand, make a raspberry sound, and then reach for the item again.

The greatest change in Ricky's communication system involved the format in which Ricky's signals were responded to or elicited. The format suggestions provided a framework to assist his communication partners at school to comprehend and respond to his signals.

Question 4: How Can Existing Signals Be Interpreted in a Consistent Manner?

Three objectives were targeted to establish consistency beyond the format changes already mentioned. They included direct training, monitoring, and providing more opportunities for making choices. Direct training of communication partners at school was provided by the teacher. She trained aides and support staff to recognize and respond to Ricky's signals in a consistent fashion. The teacher would model the presentation format and the appropriate response within existing activities. She also scheduled co-instruction with other personnel while they became familiar with the system. The teacher and the CDS worked directly with Ricky during snacktime. Classroom aides worked with Ricky during other activities such as playtime, recess, and art.

Monitoring progress was accomplished through direct observation. When Ricky used one of the recognized signals, the response of the partner was noted. Data collected by the consultant at the beginning of intervention indicated that the aides complied with Ricky's request signals about 20% of the time. At that point, their interactions consisted mainly of preventing Ricky from touching or taking dangerous items. Although they were recognizing his signal as a request, they were not allowing the signal to function as a request for the item. Instead, from Ricky's perspective, his signal sometimes made desirable items disappear. After the teacher clarified the signals and the functions that they were to serve, and after choice-making opportunities were identified in each of the routines that were taking place, the aides responded to his requests 94% of the time.

This change is largely due to an increase in the number of appropriate-choice opportunities provided by the aides. Prior to intervention, the aides provided two opportunities for choices in a 2-hour session. Two months later, they provided 16 opportunities in different contexts during a 2-hour session. At the same time, the aides continued to prevent Ricky from taking items that were dangerous.

One effect of this intervention technique was a decrease in the number of Ricky's protests. Prior to the implementation of the communication system, Ricky was observed to signal protest 26 times in a 2-hour session. Two months later, Ricky's protesting had decreased to 8 instances in 2 hours, given fairly similar activities. This illustrates how indirect manipulation of the environment surrounding a nondesired behavior affects the behavior itself. That is, often intervention efforts need to focus on the behaviors of the partners rather than the behaviors of the child.

Question 5: How Can the Program Be Designed such that Language Input Is Provided at a Level Ricky Can Readily Comprehend?

Since the assessment data indicated a reliance on gestures in addition to verbalization, it was agreed that verbal language input needed to be repetitive, simplified, and supported by gestures. Two approaches were targeted for implementation. First, the consultant suggested that salient parts of routines be marked by the use of the same word by all partners. It was hoped that this would help Ricky to establish the correspondence between words and their meaning. For example, when an activity was finished, it was recommended that the words, "All done," and a sign "FINISHED" be used. The consultant modeled this for the aides during an art activity, and the teacher monitored their interactions with Ricky on a continuing basis. After repeated exposure, Ricky may begin to understand this signal and move on to a new activity with less assistance.

The second technique was for the adults to simplify language and use gestures toward real objects as support. Many of the adults in Ricky's environment used long sentences when they were talking with him. The reason for this may have been due to a lack of awareness of Ricky's needs or even a belief that the manner of speaking to Ricky was inconsequential due to his lack of understanding. During the assessment, a marked increase in contingent behaviors was noted when simplified language, plus gestures, were used. Again, this type of language was modeled by the consultant and the teacher.

Finally, instructional videotapes were planned to show the change in Ricky's contingent behavior given complex versus simplified language. This would enable other adults to learn about Ricky's abilities and formats for enhancing his performance.

Question 6: How Can More Social Interactions Be Encouraged?

This question was partially answered by increasing the responses to Ricky's signals and the opportunities for making choices. The eye contact patterns, however, remained a concern for many of his partners at school. Ricky averted gaze in close proximity to others, attended to peers and adults from a distance, and made brief eye contact when the adult leaned back from close interaction. Classmates remarked, "He doesn't care." Adults sometimes felt that Ricky was purposely ignoring them.

At first, the staff decided to intervene with this behavior to encourage what were considered to be "more conventional patterns of visual contact." The technique included maintaining more distance when working one-on-one with Ricky and shaping an alternating gaze between the object and the adult. This was to be accomplished by, for example, presenting food choices and when Ricky looked at one, bringing the choice closer to the adult's eyes as he or she said, "This?" It was felt that this procedure would be less intrusive and more natural than a cue such as, "Look at me."

This intervention was terminated rather hastily after Ricky's cultural background was reconsidered. Ricky is a member of a northwest Native American tribe and his family practiced many of the typical cultural interaction patterns. This included the absence of direct eye contact when in close proximity, particularly with people in an authority position. After discussion regarding the "eye contact" intervention, the teacher remembered the grandmother and father using these patterns during conferences. To instruct Ricky to use a gesture that is conventional for other cultures is inappropriate, insensitive, and places a cultural bias on assessment and intervention. Efforts were made, instead, to educate his peer and adult communication partners as to Ricky's meaning of these behaviors since the potential for misinterpretation had already been demonstrated. This information is shared in an effort to increase the sensitivity of others regarding the cultural biases that may exist among education teams.

FUTURE DIRECTIONS

The next step for Ricky may be to introduce an object system wherein the object he touches is a replica of the one he will receive. An empty cup and a plastic cookie or cracker could be attached with Velcro to a small board or placed within a more portable 3 inch by 5 inch, three-ring binder. Touching one of these items will be recognized as a signal for requesting the real item. This will be implemented if he continues to make clear choices using his present system with his new teacher in kindergarten.

Maintaining consistency of input and response among his communication partners must remain a focus. The task of instructing partners and coordinating efforts was assigned to the preschool teacher. She will work with Ricky's kindergarten teacher so that this role can be passed on.

In Ricky's case, participation from home was minimal. His grandmother was willing to have the teacher try any system at school, but the system that Ricky and his grandmother had developed at home remained the same. The home system was similar to that implemented at school; however, if changes to a more symbolic level, such as an object board, occur at school, it may evolve as a school-only system. Many parents feel relieved to find a system that works and are hesitant to give it up. A videotape of Ricky successfully using a new set of symbols systems might persuade the grandmother to try the new system at home.

Finally, observations of Ricky at home with his cousins and other family members would enable school personnel to learn more about the gaze patterns mentioned. Since little specific information is available on these practices, personal observations and interviews are probably the best avenue to determine whether Ricky is using a culturally appropriate pattern of visual attention or has idiosyncratic patterns.

SUMMARY

Ricky's communication system consists of using several existing behavioral forms with familiar objects to perform functions that are already within his repertoire. The emphasis is on improving the identification of these signals by his communication partners and providing additional choice opportunities throughout his day.

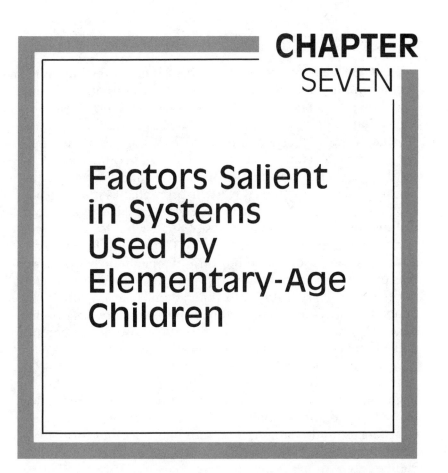

CHAPTER
SEVEN

Factors Salient in Systems Used by Elementary-Age Children

A number of factors that influence the final selection and use of a communication system become salient during the elementary years. These factors involve the age of the student, his or her potential for learning, the remaining years of educational services, and the significant roles of parents/caregivers in his or her life. These factors significantly influence the design of a communication system as a user enters and then leaves the elementary school for the next level. Consideration of these factors can assist practitioners to negotiate the preferences of all persons involved and to incorporate the compromises necessary when designing the actual system.

Each of the case histories that follow involves students in the elementary grades. Kyle is the youngest, in his first year in elementary school, while Jodi is the oldest, enrolled in her last year at the elementary level. Each of the students attends a regular public school and lives with his or her natural family. The above factors were incorporated into the final system selection and implemented in the following manner.

Each student resides at home with his or her natural family and the expectation is that he or she will continue to do so until the age of 21. Thus, the preferences and limitations that his or her family expressed were incorporated as much as possible. For instance, the system for Kyle was selected as a compromise between the preferences of the teacher for real objects and the family for photos and words. The systems for Matu and Jodi were not used at home until independent performance was observed at school; however, parents' requests and preferences were incorporated into the system. Later, as these students are introduced to different living situations, the preferences of other caregivers, in addition to those of the parents, will influence his or her communication system.

At this time, these students receive an additional 8–14 years of educational services prior to age 21. The possibility for beginning with one communication system, designed to reflect his or her cognitive abilities and current environmental circumstances, and changing to a more abstract and formal system is quite high. Therefore, the present systems reflect current abilities to a much higher degree than might occur if these students were adolescents or adults.

KYLE

NAME: Kyle
AGE: 7 years
TEACHER: Mary Moreau
CONSULTANTS: Diane
                   Baumgart
                   Carolynn
                   Leavitt

SYSTEM

Kyle used both a communication booklet and a daily schedule system. Miniature objects were used on both communication systems to represent people, objects, places, and activities.

OVERVIEW

Kyle resides with his family in a rural town with a population of 290. He developed normally until he contracted spinal meningitis at 6 months of age. After his illness, he was diagnosed as having mental retardation in the severe to profound range and a seizure disorder. His seizures have intermittently been difficult to control with medication. Kyle received educational services since he was 1 year old from, at first, a Child Development Center, and later, a university developmental preschool. Kyle traveled to these centers that were approximately 50 miles from his home. At the age of 5, he began receiving special education services and attended kindergarten in his hometown. He currently continues to receive special education services and is mainstreamed into first grade and the physical education, art, music, and library classes with his peers. An outline of his developmental profile follows.

INFORMATION FROM SCHOOL RECORDS

The information from school records includes Kyle's status in cognition, motor skills, vision and hearing, speech and language, and behavior.

Cognition

Past assessments indicated that Kyle's cognitive level was at 18–24 months in the following areas: problem solving, vocal and motor imitation, object differentiation, object permanence, visual discrimination, prereading, and math skills.

In problem-solving skills, Kyle reproduces actions with simple toys, appeals to an adult for specific actions (e.g., hugs, eat, drink) and persists with 2 or more strategies to obtain a desired object (e.g., climbs on chairs, moves barriers). Anecdotal reports from his current teacher, aides, and parents indicated that his abilities may include sight word recognition and visual discrimination of photos.

Motor Skills

Kyle can easily navigate around different objects in his environment using a heel-to-toe gait. He can walk a balance beam with some assistance, jump on both feet, and balance on one foot for 5 seconds. He climbs stairs using a right-to-left foot progression; however, he is supervised on stairs and in the playground due to seizures. Kyle can throw a ball overhand, but not to a target or person. He does not squat in play or to recover items. Developmentally, Kyle's gross motor abilities range from 3–4 years of age in the area of dynamic balance, 2–3 years for static balance, and at approximately 10 months for upper extremity gross motor skills.

Fine motor skills include full range of motion with both arms and hands. He utilizes an inferior or superior pincer grasp on objects of various sizes. Kyle places and releases objects on a large surface and places objects in containers. He does not button or use a zipper. He can use a fork to stab food and a spoon to scoop with 50% accuracy with both. Previous assessment indicated that developmentally, Kyle's fine motor abilities ranged from 9–12 months. Currently, his ability is approximately in the 24–30 month range.

Vision and Hearing

No vision exam has been conducted and no serious vision problem has been suspected. A hearing exam was scheduled but not completed within the time interval of this case history.

Speech and Language

Kyle says a few words such as "Hi there," "Well, come here," and "No." He also sings a few songs such as "Happy Birthday" and "Twinkle, Twinkle, Little Star." Other vocalizations are incomprehensible to his teachers and parents but they are used with a variety of intonations.

Past assessments indicated that Kyle communicates to greet, to obtain attention and objects, and to terminate or refuse. Previously, Kyle was reported to sign the following words with some physical assistance: "want," "more," "eat," "drink," "go," and "open." Currently, Kyle signs "eat" and "more" spontaneously on rare occasions, but still requires physical assistance to sign "want," "drink," "go," and "open."

Behavior

Kyle responds well to praise and encouragement and attempts to please significant others. When frustrated by attempts to obtain a desired object or by the difficulty of a task, Kyle acts out by hitting, scratching, kicking, or biting.

ASSESSMENT FOR COMMUNICATION SYSTEM PLANNING

Prior to the design and implementation of an augmentative system, a number of additional assessments were required in order to design an individualized system. These questions of concerns, assessment procedures, and conclusions are described below.

Question 1: What Are Kyle's Cognitive Abilities?

Reports from Kyle's parents and teachers varied greatly with the assessments on file. Examples of his abilities were provided that indicated that he was able to match photos with printed words and make fairly complex visual discriminations. The assessments on file indicated that he was unable to perform simple discriminations or to follow 3-word requests. The question of concern was whether these differences in written and verbal reports were perceptions of different observers or whether his ability level actually varied at times.

Assessments Assessments were conducted on object permanence, matching skills, and visual discrimination. Assessments were completed throughout a 4-month period of time through informal observations and formal test situations. Assessment of object permanence included visible and invisible displacement of favorite objects, including food items and toys, and were conducted both at home and at school. Visible displacement was conducted formally by showing Kyle a desired toy or food item which was then hidden under a cloth. Kyle watched as the item was taken from under the cloth and hidden under a second cloth. Invisible displacement was conducted in the same manner; however, Kyle did not observe as the object was hidden under the second cloth.

Informal assessment data were collected anecdotally by asking adults to put items that Kyle liked in different places and to note whether or not he searched for them. For example, his mother moved the cheese from the typical drawer in the refrigerator to a shelf above the drawer where it was hidden from view.

Matching was completed with familiar toys and favorite foods. Two objects were placed side by side, visible to Kyle. A picture, a miniature object, or a full-size object similar to one of the two objects was shown to Kyle. He was then asked, "Find one like this." The objects were placed in various locations, to the left and right of midline and center. Similar testing was conducted during regular routines with familiar items of both high and low preference. For example, at lunch, a piece of cheese was shown to Kyle. He was then asked to find the same item on his lunch tray when other items were present.

Results Kyle located visibly and invisibly displaced items at 100% accuracy (i.e., 20 trials, during formal test situations, searching for items when they were and were not in their typical places). During test situations, Kyle matched objects correctly with 54% accuracy (i.e., 39 trials), pictures to objects with 59% accuracy (i.e., 34 trials), and miniatures of objects with 62% accuracy (i.e., 45 trials). During regular routines, Kyle matched two familiar objects in their usual locations with 75% accuracy. The objects used were pieces of cheese and a radio. The results indicated that Kyle did perform better on certain days. These changes were thought to be due to an occasional abatement of seizures. The performance on seemingly more difficult tasks, such as matching photos with the printed word, were observed by the consultants. These observations confirmed that Kyle's correct responses on more difficult tasks were due to inadvertently placing the correct stimulus either closer to Kyle or on his left side. When this factor was corrected by random presentation of objects, photos, or words, he was unable to accurately perform the task. This information is mentioned here to highlight the importance of both assessing for hand preference and ensuring that materials are presented randomly.

Conclusions An estimate of Kyle's typical cognitive level was from 12–24 months. This ability level is characterized by a reliance on context, verbal, and gestural cues to comprehend spoken language. Abstract symbols for language are typically not readily understood.

Question 2: What Pragmatic Intents Does Kyle Exhibit in Familiar Settings and Routines, and What Are His Receptive Communication Skills?

Assessment Kyle was observed across familiar routines to determine which types of gestures, vocalizations, and other behaviors he used to communicate. He was observed by a consultant and classroom aide on 7 days from November through February. Observers recorded the time, location, and frequency of the communicative intents. A record was made of these intents, which were categorized into six major communicative areas: makes a request or asks a question; gives an answer or responds to a question or request; describes events or aspects of the environment; expresses facts, beliefs, attitudes, or emotions; attempts to or does establish or maintain interpersonal contact or interaction; and attempts to entertain others. These categories are variations of those used by Dore (1974, 1975). A sample data sheet used for pragmatic assessments is contained in the Appendix (see Appendix A.8, Pragmatic Intent Observation Data).

In addition to these categories, receptive vocabulary was assessed in both familiar routines and test situations with preferred and nonpreferred items. Tests were conducted with the following familiar and preferred objects: cheese, cottage cheese, chips, hot dogs, pants, coat, and shoes. He was also tested on familiar commands such as "sit down," "come here," and "give me." In regular routines, Kyle was asked to show or get an item when at least two items were visible. Adults were careful to not use gestures while making requests of Kyle. For example, during lunch, Kyle was asked to pick up the cheese when other favorite items were on his tray. When getting ready to go home, he was asked to get his coat when other items were hanging on the coat rack. In formal test situations, two items were placed on a table in front of Kyle. The tester then asked Kyle to pick up a specific object, by saying, "Kyle, pick up the cheese." In all assessments, Kyle had two choices that were paired as follows: two preferred items and two nonpreferred items. This ensured that he did not select an item because it was preferred over others when it was requested.

Results Kyle used all pragmatic intents with the exception of describing events or aspects of his environment. A summary of some of the data is included in Figure 7.1 (see Appendix A.8 for a blank form).

During the 7 days of data collection, 321 incidences of pragmatic intent were observed and recorded in the following categories:

Gives an answer or responds to a question or request (36%)
Attempts to and does establish or maintain interpersonal contact or interaction (34%)
Expresses facts, beliefs, attitudes, or emotions (19%)
Makes a request; asks a question (7%)
Attempts to entertain or tease others (4%)

Pragmatic Intent Observation Data

Name: Kyle   Date: 11/17/89   Observer: _____ B.A.

Categories	Location/time/frequency	Example of activity and interpretation (write up third example observed)	Other comments
1. Makes a request; asks a question	1. Gets coat 6 times today throughout day 2. Pulls hand toward object 3 times throughout day	1. Went to get his coat at a request to go outside 2. Pulled observer's hand toward his radio and cheese 2 times	
2. Gives an answer or responds to a question or request	1. Classroom, 3 times 2. Classroom, 3 times throughout day	1. Requested to get shoes 2. Requested to get coat, responded by getting coat	
3. Describes events or aspects of the environment			
4. Expresses facts, beliefs, attitudes, or emotions	1. Swings, 2 times today 2. Toilets, 3 times 3. Lunchroom, 2 times	1. Smiled and laughed while swinging on the swing 2. Cried, hit, and attempted to bite when being taken to the toilet 3. Laughed and smiled as familiar teacher and his sister came into the cafeteria	
5. Attempts to and does establish or maintain interpersonal contact or interaction	1. Storytime, 2 times 2. Classroom, 3 times throughout day 3. Classroom, 6 times throughout day	1. Attempted to touch other children, made loud noises to draw attention to himself 2. When speech therapist and other teachers walked into the room, Kyle looked at them and said, "Hi" 3. Attempted to engage in interactions by handing toys to teacher, touching arms and faces	
6. Attempts to entertain or tease others	1. Storytime, 1 time	1. During storytime, Kyle made loud noises, the rest of the children looked, Kyle smiled, then he laughed and made more loud noises	

Figure 7.1. Sample of pragmatic intent observation data for Kyle.

Kyle made requests by pulling the observer's hand to a desired object, crying, getting an object that is required for an activity, or going to where the activity is typically performed. Kyle responded to a question or request most frequently by following one-step verbal requests with gestures; "sit down," "come here," "point to . . . ," and "hand me ." Kyle also responded to two- or three-step commands within the context of an established routine. For example, when asked to get his blanket and lie down for a nap, Kyle responded appropriately. If requested to do something he didn't like to do (e.g., go to the bathroom, go in from recess), he protested by crying, hitting, kicking, or pushing people or objects away. In fact, once this behavior was viewed as communication, it was clear to the teaching staff that Kyle clearly expressed himself and they hypothesized that the intensity of his actions might be due to his frustration at not being "heard." The actions used in the category of interacting with others typically consisted of vocalizing, "Hi there," handing items to people, hugging or grasping the observer's arm or hand, or by singing "Twinkle, Twinkle, Little Star," "Happy Birthday," or the theme from "Jeopardy." Kyle expressed emotions by smiling, singing, laughing, touching, and hugging others when happy; crying when sad or hurt; and screaming, hitting, crying, kicking, and biting when angry. He entertained others by singing. He also teased his brother by taking a toy and waiting until his brother chased him to get the toy. The teasing category is difficult to separate from that of interacting with others. The observers felt strongly, however, that these actions were teasing.

In the area of receptive communication, Kyle most frequently responded to requests to "come here," "point to . . . ," and "give me . . . ." In addition, within familiar routines such as lunch or going to the store, Kyle retrieved the following items when they were requested: eggs, cheese, chips, cottage cheese, pants, coat, hat, and shoes. Kyle did not retrieve these items when named and requested outside the context of an established routine when they were either in or out of sight. During formal testing for receptive vocabulary, Kyle picked up or touched the object that was named 52% of the time when two familiar items were present. This is slightly above the chance level of 50%. During established routines, he followed two- or three-step directions. He was not able to follow similar requests when the context was changed. A sample of the data collected is presented in Figure 7.2 (see Appendix A.9 for a blank form).

Conclusions Kyle was observed to communicate his needs through all areas of pragmatic intent with the exception of describing events or aspects of the environment. The communication system chosen should try to incorporate his existing intents using symbols more readily understood by teachers, his parents, siblings, and classmates. His teachers examined the

Basic Receptive Language Assessment Form

Name:　　Kyle　　　　Date:　　2–15–89　　　　Observer:　　Carolynn

Instructions:　Present two objects to the student. Name one of the objects and ask the student to point to it, look at it, or use it (any of these responses is acceptable). Place an "X" in the appropriate column for the student's response. Complete at least 10 trials, varying the objects and the position of their presentation.

Objects presented	Object requested	Student's response Correct	Student's response Incorrect
Cheese/orange	Cheese		X
Hotdog/orange	Orange		X
Soda/orange	Soda	X	
Cottage cheese/hotdog	Hotdog	X	X
Orange/cheese	Cheese		X
Soda/cheese	Cheese		X
Cheese/hotdog	Cheese	X	
Cottage cheese/cheese	Cottage cheese	X	
Orange/cheese	Cheese		X
Hotdog/cheese	Cheese	X	
Hotdog/soda	Soda	X	
Cottage cheese/hotdog	Cottage cheese	X	
Hotdog/cottage cheese	Hotdog	X	
Cottage cheese/orange	Orange	X	
Cottage cheese/cheese	Cottage cheese		X
Soda/cottage cheese	Soda		X
Cottage cheese/orange	Cottage cheese		X
Cottage cheese/hotdog	Hotdog	X	

Comments: Kyle does not scan from item to item; however, the observer believes that often Kyle chooses the item he would like as opposed to the object shown or requested.

Figure 7.2.　Data collected using the Basic Receptive Language Assessment Form.

pragmatic intents and were able to list vocabulary words for some of his actions. His requests were primarily for "drink." He responded to requests or questions from others by tantruming and saying, "No," or by performing the actions requested. Interacting with others was performed by saying, "Hi there," and smiling, or by singing, making eye contact, and smiling. The vocabulary words "drink" and "no" were selected for first words. His present means of interacting with people by smiling, touching, and so forth, and expressing emotions by crying, smiling, or other actions were deemed appropriate for the present and staff decided that these should be reinforced more consistently. Context and routines were important cues that helped Kyle understand verbal communication. The communication system selected should be used and taught within the context of a routine until mastery is reached, rather than at a desk top using repeated trials of a task for instructing.

Question 3: What Visual Tracking and Scanning Skills Can Kyle Use and How Should the Layout of His System be Designed to Utilize His Present Skills?

No previous assessments had been conducted and this information is critical in selecting the presentation format and array of a communication system. The procedures outlined in Chapter Five were used for these assessments.

Assessments Tracking was assessed through informal observation and formal test procedures. A variety of preferred objects such as small toys, food items, and a flashlight were used. Kyle was required to follow the moving object horizontally and vertically, at eye level, above and below eye level, and to the left and right of midline. Scanning was assessed through informal observation and formal testing using matching tasks in which Kyle was required to scan two objects to find the one that was requested. Sample visual tracking data collected are included in Figure 7.3 (see Appendix A.4 for a blank form).

Results Kyle was able to track an object in all directions. He stopped tracking an object more often when it was above his eye level. Kyle did not scan between two objects during

Visual Tracking Data Sheet

Name: Kyle   Date: 2-8-89

Observer: Carolynn L.   Materials Used: flashlight, small toys, food

Instructions: Using objects that the individual will readily watch, begin at the appropriate reference point (indicated by the letters and boxes) and move the object along the designated visual plane. Watch the individual's eyes during tracking and indicate whether the tracking was continuous or interrupted. Also record if there were any indications of nystagmus or strabismus.

Tracking	Continuous	Interrupted
Horizontal, above eye level: (A to B and B to A)		x Interrupted
Horizontal, at eye level: (C to D and D to C)	x Continuous	
Horizontal, below eye level: (E to F and F to E)	x Continuous	
Vertical (at midline): (G to H and H to G)	x Continuous	
Diagonal: (A to F and F to A)	x Continuous	
Diagonal: (B to E and E to B)	x Continuous	

Nystagmus (bouncing eyes): _____ Right _____ Left _____ Both

Strabismus (eyes turn in/out): _____ Right _____ Left _____ Both

Comments: Sometimes tracked by moving head.

Figure 7.3. Sample data collected on visual tracking for Kyle.

matching tasks. He answered the cue, "Point to . . ." by typically looking down or away from the objects and touching one of them. It was reported by classroom aides and other observers that Kyle scanned to find a desired object. For example, he would visually inspect items in the cupboard to find chips.

Conclusions The presentation of communication symbols should be at or below eye level. Scanning skills need to be taught or required if more than one symbol is presented simultaneously. Since it appears that Kyle can scan but does not do so, a forced time-delay between presentation and selection may be required to encourage and require scanning and to help eliminate selecting prior to looking.

Question 4: What Is Kyle's Hand Preference and Functional Hand Usage? What Motor Responses Could Kyle Use to Attract Attention to His Communication System?

This information is necessary when selecting a physical means for indicating preferences (e.g., sign language, representational pictures/objects) and for the placement of his communication system.

Assessments Hand preference and usage were observed during classroom activities, informal play, lunchtime routines, and matching activities where Kyle was required to grasp and point to objects placed at midline and to the right and left of the center while sitting at a table or standing. A data sheet with sample data is contained in Figure 7.4 (see Appendix A.6 for a blank data sheet).

Results Kyle used his left hand to manipulate objects and to grasp utensils while eating. He used his left hand to complete most reaching and grasping activities and crossed midline to pick up an object placed to his right. However, crossing midline was not consistently performed. The data revealed that he used his right hand 30% of the time to obtain objects on his right, rather than crossing midline with his left (preferred) hand. Kyle used his whole hand when pointing spontaneously, and required a physical prompt to point with his index finger.

Conclusions Kyle prefers to use his left hand for most tasks but occasionally uses his right hand seemingly to avoid crossing midline. Objects should be placed on his left side, and use of his fingers to point or make signs will probably require considerable physical assistance.

Data Sheet for Assessing Hand Preference

Date: _____2/8/89_____ Observer: _____Carolynn_____

Name:_____Kyle_____ Time: throughout the day_____

Materials used: _____food items, toys_____

Which hand is used to pick up objects when the object is placed in the following locations in relation to the body? Put an X in the blank which describes the hand used.

Left front   Right front

                              Middle

Left side   Right side

                          Student
                          is here
                     facing forward

Sitting at a table:

Left front:	L hand	X		R hand	
Left side:	L hand	X		R hand	
Middle:	L hand	X		R hand	
Right front:	L hand			R hand	X
Right side:	L hand	X		R hand	

Standing:

Left front:	L hand	X		R hand	
Left side:	L hand	X		R hand	
Middle:	L hand	X		R hand	
Right front:	L hand	X		R hand	
Right side:	L hand	X		R hand	

Figure 7.4. Sample data collected on Kyle's hand preference.

Summary of Results Used in Selecting a System

It was determined by the parents and teaching staff that a communication system should be selected for three purposes, including:

1. Provide a means for Kyle to indicate negation (i.e., "no") in a variety of situations. Thus, "no" was selected as a vocabulary word.
2. Provide a means for Kyle to indicate his requests. Since he enjoys getting a drink and it can occur frequently during the day and across school, home, and community settings, "drink" was selected as a vocabulary word.
3. Provide a means for staff and parents to tell Kyle what is to happen next using more than the current spoken language. The instructional team thought this might assist Kyle to "know" what was expected of him, what was to occur next, and, thus, might eliminate the tantrums (e.g., crying, hitting, biting) that occurred when transitions to activities outside of his classroom took place. For example, Kyle likes to go to recess and swing, an activity that involves leaving the classroom. However, going to all other school environments and activities (e.g., physical education, first grade, bathroom, cafeteria, music, library) require this same initial route and he tantrums when he realizes that he is not going to the recess grounds.

In reviewing the purposes listed above, examining the assessment information, and determining Kyle's signing skills to date, the staff and his parents felt that the communication system needed to be as concrete as possible to enhance communication. The system also needed to be designed for use during days when seizures had abated as well as on days when they were a problem. Sign language was determined to be too abstract for Kyle. The team discussed the use of actual objects and miniature objects. Complete agreement on "the best" system was not reached, but the team decided to try a miniature object system to "see how Kyle did." This system was smaller and more portable, and thus its use at home and school seemed more likely. It also was more acceptable than objects to Kyle's parents and extended family. Finally, Kyle's "looking away" behavior was discussed. Although it interfered with intentional selection, and was considered a problem "to be looked into," it was felt that a system that did not require Kyle to scan should be initially designed. The team felt that minimizing demands of

Kyle would minimize frustration and enable him to focus on communication.

SYSTEM'S ACTUAL DESIGN

A 3 inch by 5 inch, three-ring binder was designed as part of Kyle's actual communication system so that it could attach to Kyle's belt. Two pages were inserted into the binder with the symbols "No" and "Drink" on them. Since a miniature for "No" was not readily available, a circle with a line through it, as in "No Smoking," was used. Data were not collected on his use of "No." A schedule of his school days, represented by miniatures and attached to index cards, was also designed. This schedule board was attached to a wall in his classroom. A separate schedule board reflecting times at home was made. Some of the miniatures used and the layout of his schedule system at home are shown in Figure 7.5(a & b). His communication booklet is shown in Figure 7.6.

The initial objectives for teaching Kyle to use the schedule and communication boards are listed below. Objectives were altered (as noted on Figures 7.6 and 7.7) after instruction began (see pages 156 and 158).

1. Schedule board objective. Given the verbal cue, "What's next?," Kyle will, with gestural and verbal prompts, walk to the schedule board, choose the first card on the left, and go to the activity. He will do this given only gestural and verbal prompts for every activity, each day, for three data collection days. Data will be taken twice per week.
2. Communication board objective. If Kyle indicates that he wants _____ during an activity, the teacher will say, "Kyle, yes, you want _____" and point to the _____ in his book. The teacher then says, "Kyle, show me the _____ in your book." His communication book will be positioned for him and he will point to the _____. Kyle will do this given only gestural and verbal prompts throughout two consecutive weeks, for each communication item (e.g., drink, cheese, radio).

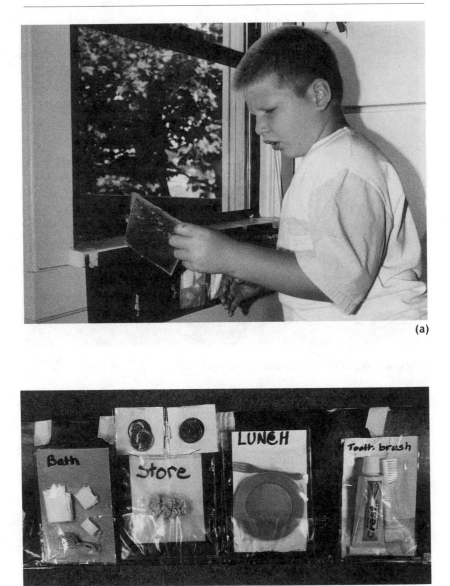

Figure 7.5. (a) Example of Kyle using his schedule system at home; (b) Sample of miniatures used for Kyle.

Figure 7.6. Kyle's communication booklet.

A least-to-most level of prompting was used during instruction, and procedural data (i.e., data on the level of assistance needed to perform) were collected two times a week for the schedule board and a minimum of once per week for his communication book. The levels of the prompts used were:

Level 1: No instructional cues or prompts
Level 2: Indirect verbal prompt
Level 3: Indirect verbal prompt and point
Level 4: Indirect verbal prompt and physical prompt
Level 5: Direct verbal cue
Level 6: Direct verbal cue and point
Level 7: Direct verbal cue and physical prompt
Level 8: Direct verbal cue and perform action for student

Data were collected by the aides and/or a student teacher. For graphing purposes, the prompts given to Kyle were marked with a: "+" if they were a verbal and gestural prompt, verbal prompt, or independent; and "−" if they were a model or physical prompt. Procedural data enabled the staff to determine if Kyle was requiring less intrusive prompts (i.e., a model of what to do rather than physical assistance to perform).

EFFECTIVENESS OF THE SYSTEM

The schedule board has proved to be effective in helping Kyle to anticipate transitions and in providing extra cues for what activity was next. For example, prior to the implementation of the schedule board, when Kyle left the classroom, he usually anticipated going to recess. If recess was not the next activity, Kyle would tantrum when redirected. These tantrums dissipated with the implementation of the schedule board. In addition, the schedule board enabled staff to more clearly understand Kyle's preferences. When the "restroom" card was "next" on the schedule, Kyle usually responded with whining and crying. Since it had been hypothesized earlier that he did not like this activity and since this behavior was seen only with the "restroom" card, the staff were convinced of both his dislike and his ability to associate the card with its referent activity. The schedule cards were effective when Kyle needed to travel some distance to the activity (e.g., the post office, stores) because the cards were small (i.e., 3 inches by 5 inches) and could be carried as an additional reminder of the destination. Because Kyle does not scan between items, the schedule board activities were lined up from left to right. Before beginning an activity and after the cue had been given, Kyle would go to the schedule board. He would choose the corresponding activity card that was always the first card on the left. The activity card would not be returned to the schedule board once the activity was finished. The next activity chosen was then the first activity card on the left of the schedule board, thereby eliminating the need for Kyle to scan to find the correct activity. Data were collected by an aide and a student teacher twice a week. A summary of progress data is included in Figure 7.7. Interrat-

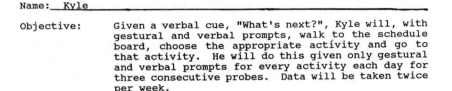

Name: __Kyle__

Objective: Given a verbal cue, "What's next?", Kyle will, with
               gestural and verbal prompts, walk to the schedule
               board, choose the appropriate activity and go to
               that activity. He will do this given only gestural
               and verbal prompts for every activity each day for
               three consecutive probes. Data will be taken twice
               per week.

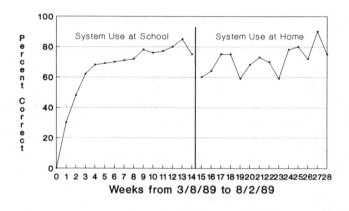

Key: Correct • Verbal, gestural, and independent performance
     Incorrect • Physical or modeling prompts

Figure 7.7.   Summary of data on the use of the schedule board.

er reliability data were collected six times from March through
May. Interrater reliability ranged from 86%–100%, with a
mean of 94.6%.

Prior to implementing the communication system in a
portable book, two communication cards (i.e., "Drink" and
"No") were positioned above the sink where Kyle had access
to them. The "Drink" card used a miniature glass with the
word "Drink" printed on it. The "No" card was shown in
Figure 7.6. Throughout the day, opportunities to request a
drink were increased by taking Kyle to the sink or bubbler
areas more frequently. His cup at the sink was out of reach and
he needed assistance to activate the bubbler. Thus, when Kyle
touched, pointed, looked at, or pulled the teacher's hand to
make a request, she responded by saying, "Yes, you want a

drink?" Kyle then was assisted to select the "Drink" card. He quickly mastered this and needed no assistance. The communication cards "No" and "Drink" were then incorporated into a small 3 inch by 5 inch book that was attached to his belt. Kyle required physical assistance to position the book and to turn the pages. He was again given increased opportunities to request assistance throughout the school day, and began to find the drink page on his own. The communication system was then expanded by adding additional items (e.g., cheese, toilet, radio). The data indicated that Kyle rarely refused a drink and by adding additional items could indicate "No" when the teacher offered an item he hadn't chosen. A summary of progress is contained in Figure 7.8. Interrater reliability data was collected six times throughout the months of February, March, and April and ranged from 91%–100%, with a mean of 97%.

SUMMARY

The communication system used by Kyle was implemented in the school environment only, during February through June, 1989. For the months of June through August, 1989, Kyle received educational services through the extended school year program. A similar communication system was developed for Kyle's home environment during this time. A schedule board for morning and evening routines was used along with his communication book with the words: drink, cheese, no, and radio. Currently, Kyle requires gestural and verbal prompts to use his schedule board and communication book at home. It is recommended that once Kyle reaches criterion performance at this prompt level, it should be faded to the use of a verbal prompt, then natural cues only.

Kyle's communication book is formatted so that only one item is visible at a time. In order to assist Kyle to scan, it is recommended that once criterion performance has been achieved with his current system, the array of items should be altered so that two are visible simultaneously. Kyle would then be required to scan between the two items to indicate which

Name: _Kyle_

Objective 1: Kyle indicates he wants a drink by turning on the water, and given a verbal cue, "Do you want a drink?", Kyle will indicate "yes" by choosing the "drink" card when the cards, "drink" and "no," are positioned above the sink. He will do this with only verbal and gestural prompts for two weeks.

Objective 2: Given a model cue, "Point to the _____," and a verbal cue, "Kyle, show me the _____," and his communication book held for him and open to the page of _____, Kyle will point to the _____. He will do this given verbal and gestural prompts over two consecutive weeks for each communication item; drink, cheese, and radio.

Objective 3: Given a verbal cue, "Kyle, what do you want? Show me in your book," when he indicates he wants/doesn't want radio, restroom, cheese, drink and given his book, held for him, Kyle will turn the pages to the _____ and point to the _____. He will do this, given only verbal prompts, for each trial for three consecutive weeks for each page; no, cheese, drink, and radio.

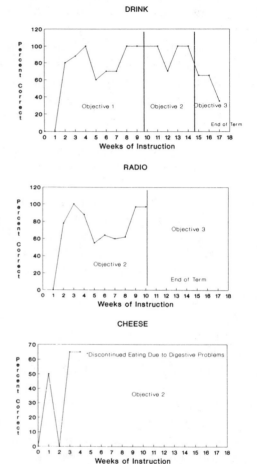

Figure 7.8. Summary of data on the use of the communication system.

item was desired. In addition, Kyle's present schedule board system does not require him to scan to find the correct item. It is further recommended that once criterion performance has been achieved in his current system, that he return the schedule card to the schedule board upon completion of the activity. This will require him to scan to find the empty slot and to locate the next activity card, rather than simply choosing the activity card on the left as his current system requires.

MATU

NAME: Matu
AGE: 8 years
TEACHER: Peggy Scuderi
CONSULTANTS: Diane Baumgart, Brent Askvig, Ed Helmstetter
COMMUNICATIONS DISORDERS SPECIALIST: Chris Englehart

SYSTEM

This case history describes the assessment process and development of a daily activity picture schedule for an elementary student with autism. Data on the effectiveness of the schedule system are included and considerations for future communication systems are discussed.

OVERVIEW

Matu resides with both parents, an older brother, and a younger brother in a small north Idaho community. His family and he have previously lived in Canada for 3 years and prior to that, lived in Africa. His father is a graduate student in college and his mother is a housewife. Matu has been diagnosed as having autism. Moderate or severe mental retardation is also suspected, but this has not been confirmed due to difficulty in testing (see Cognition section for details on the testing). Matu was placed in a self-contained special education class in an elementary school at age 7. Prior to this placement, Matu had not received any special education or other related services. Approximately 15 students received services from the special education teacher. Matu, like all students in the class, was mainstreamed into age-appropriate classrooms for at least one class period each day. This was a music or physical education class. A classroom aide assisted Matu in all activities.

INFORMATION FROM SCHOOL RECORDS

The information that follows includes Matu's status from the school records on cognition, motor skills, vision and hearing, speech and language, social interaction, and behavior.

162

Cognition

Matu's records contained no formal assessment of his cognitive abilities. The teacher and the Communication Disorders Specialist (CDS) noted that all attempts at formal cognitive assessment had failed because Matu did not comply with the basic commands necessary for most intellectual assessments.

Motor Skills

There were no indications of gross motor or fine motor deficits or delays either from formal tests or upon observation.

Vision and Hearing

No visual deficits were noted. However, the teacher expressed concern about Matu's lack of eye contact with peers. He also shifted his gaze away from adults but would then turn and watch them when they were not looking at him. In addition, Matu's teacher indicated that he had trouble scanning pictures and generally needed verbal prompting and pointing to assist him in this task. Although Matu often did not carry out verbal requests, his hearing was assumed to be within normal limits. No formal hearing assessment results were present in his file.

Speech and Language

While Matu was capable of somewhat complex verbal productions in the appropriate contexts (e.g., "I want shoes to put on"), he would generally use nonverbal means (e.g., eye gaze, running away, turning away) to communicate. At times, he would speak in two- or three-word sentences and would frequently imitate statements that the teacher or his aide had just made. Frequently he would speak after a request from an adult was directed to him or if he was frustrated with others who did not correctly interpret his nonverbal messages.

Matu's receptive and expressive communication abilities were measured using the communication section of the Topeka Association for Retarded Citizens (TARC) assessment system (Sailor & Mix, 1975), and yielded the following results: expressive language, standard score of 40; receptive language, standard score of 50; and pre-academic communication skills, standard score of 60. The overall communication section standard score was 55. When compared to the norming group for the TARC, which was 3–16-year-old students with moderate or severe disabilities, Matu's scores were within the average range of performance for that group (i.e., mean 50, standard deviation 20). That is, Matu's performance on the TARC was typical of other students with a similar degree of disability. Examples of the skills for which Matu received credit in the assessment included the ability to follow some directions, use some understandable words, match objects and pictures, and recite some simple songs. No other speech and language assessment information was available.

Social Interaction

On the social skills section and the observed behavior subsection of the TARC, Matu received a standard score of 30. On the pre-academic social skills subsection, he received a standard score of 27. The overall social skills standard score was 30. He was noted to have difficulty with consistently following directions and interacting with peers or adults. He showed a strength in the basic pre-academic classroom skills area (e.g., showing happiness when parent returns, not eating nonedible substances, seeking attention when needing help).

Along with the information from the TARC, the classroom teacher completed an informal, social interaction observation of Matu. She noted that he rarely interacted with peers in the classroom or at recess, but instead, preferred to be around adults. He would most frequently interact with adults in structured classroom situations. Often, teacher prompts and specific reinforcement were required to maintain the interactions. During play, Matu would remain within the same space and with the same materials as his peers, but he would not interact with them. He did not imitate the play actions or verbal productions of his peers or demonstrate awareness of their actions.

Behavior

Matu's file contained considerable information on his behavior in structured and unstructured school activities. Most of the teacher's notes concerned the responses Matu exhibited when he was asked to perform tasks. In these situations, Matu would look away from, or gaze passively at, the adult or peer who made the request, run away from the activity, whine, hum, flick his fingers against a person or object, throw himself on the floor, or jump up and down continuously while laughing. When he was removed from an activity or situation that he enjoyed, he might run, cling to the adult, or masturbate. Occasionally, Matu would also remove his clothing and run away. These behaviors appeared to occur most frequently when Matu was exposed to new classroom activities or new foods, when he made a transition from one activity to another, or when he moved from one classroom area or aide/teacher to another.

Matu's parents indicated that he preferred to play by himself at home. If left unattended outdoors, Matu would often run away from his parents or siblings. If he did not want to participate in an activity with family members, he would look away from them, leave the area, or tantrum. His parents reported that he often had one or two tantrums each day on the weekends.

The teacher completed the Motivation Assessment Scale (MAS) (Durand & Crimmins, 1988), for Matu's most frequent noncompliant behavior, passive gaze. The results indicated that Matu used the passive gaze as an "escape" function. That is, he exhibited the passive gaze either to ignore requests to perform certain tasks or to remove himself from situations.

ASSESSMENT FOR COMMUNICATION SYSTEM PLANNING

Because Matu's behaviors were not conducive to instruction for him or his classmates, the CDS was consulted. It was decided that some type of communication system might be an effective means of allowing Matu to deal with classroom changes and providing him with a more stable learning environment. Before selecting a communication system, further information was gathered about the nature and levels of Matu's communicative behavior and its functions. Data were collected on his spontaneous speech in a variety of settings and on his matching abilities. In addition, an analysis of settings in which Matu needed a more formal means of communication was completed. The specific questions regarding these factors, along with the assessment results, are presented below.

Question 1: What Types of Behavior Does Matu Utilize for Communication and What Are the Pragmatic Intents of the Behaviors?

Assessments Two informal interview/observation instruments were used to analyze the purposes of Matu's communicative behaviors. They included an observation tool for analyzing the communicative functions of behavior (Donnellan et al., 1984) and a communication interview (Schuler, Peck, Willard, & Theimer, 1989). Both instruments list several behaviors (e.g., crying, aggression, gesturing, speech approximations) that individuals may use to communicate, along with a variety of possible communicative functions of the behaviors (e.g., requesting objects, initiating interactions, declaring feelings). For each of the communicative functions listed on the instruments, a check mark is placed under the behavior that is thought to serve that specific function. For example, if the observer notes that the individual appears to cry to get someone to pay attention to him or her, then a check mark is placed under the column "cry" in the row denoted "requesting attention." The communication functions assessment was completed by the teacher and the CDS after observing Matu in a variety of school settings and interactions opportunities. The communication interview was completed by the teacher and Matu's mother during a parent-teacher conference.

Results The results of the above assessments indicated that Matu used several behaviors for a variety of pragmatic intents. The results indicated that when Matu interacted with adults, he most frequently used facial expressions, physical proximity to the adult, and passive gaze to either initiate or terminate interactions. When an adult failed to immediately respond to Matu's verbal or nonverbal requests, he would cling to the adult, flick his fingers on him or her, whine, or cry to get the person to respond to him. Matu used facial expressions (e.g., squinting his eyes, smiling) and object manipulations (e.g., holding on to objects, turning them over repetitively, holding them out to an adult) as requests for the adult to perform some type of action. For example, Matu would bring a toy to an adult and smile, and hold the toy up to have him or her turn it on for him. When he did not want to do something, he would tantrum (e.g., fall on the floor and scream), run from the person or activity, or cry and whine continuously. Matu expressed his feelings with facial expressions (e.g., smiling, squinting, frowning) or by staying close to and hugging an adult. He would tantrum, cry, or run away to protest if routines were changed or if he was required to participate in an activity in which he did not wish to be involved.

Conclusions Matu uses a variety of nonverbal behaviors to communicate his intents, including smiles, passive gaze, running away, and tantrums. He uses the behaviors to initiate interactions, to terminate interactions, to request actions or objects from adults, or to gain the attention of an adult. These behaviors are disruptive to the other students, difficult to accurately interpret, and often interrupt instruction.

Question 2: What Are Matu's Conceptual Matching Abilities?

Assessments A series of informal matching tasks, based upon the perceptual categories and subtests outlined by Schuler (1980), was developed to examine Matu's conceptual abilities. These tasks assessed his ability to match identical objects, similar objects, partial and complete objects, component parts of objects, functionally related objects, photographs and objects, and line drawings and objects. The information obtained on Matu's performance of these matching tasks assisted the teacher and CDS in determining the appropriate level of conceptual complexity for his communication system. While the results of such tasks do not provide specific cognitive or conceptual developmental levels, they do provide an indication of an individual's ability to handle various levels of abstraction as the tasks are arranged from least to most abstract. Thus, the level of abstraction (e.g., real object, photograph, line drawing) at which a student can conceptually match or discriminate objects can be identified.

Matu performed the matching tasks while seated across a table from the teacher. The items used were objects that he used in the classroom, such as books and crayons, or ones that he typically used for daily living skills, such as shoes and washcloths. For each task, the two objects were placed in front of him and a verbal cue was provided (e.g., "Find the same one," "What goes with this?"). Matu then pointed to an object or placed two objects next to each other in response to the cues.

Results   Matu correctly matched 75% of the sets of identical classroom objects (e.g., cards, blocks, crayons). When presented with two similar objects (e.g., two different colored blocks, two types of cups), he correctly matched them 75% of the time. Matu was only able to match partial objects to complete objects (e.g., broken cup to whole cup) with 50% accuracy, but did match component parts of objects (e.g., bottle and bottle cap, shoe and shoelace) with 100% accuracy. Finally, he correctly matched 75% of the sets of functionally related objects such as a paintbrush and paints and a washcloth and soap. When presented with a photograph or line drawing and a set of two objects, Matu correctly matched the photos or drawings to the objects with 90% accuracy. The teacher noted that he would collect and line up the line drawings that he correctly matched, but readily handed all of the photographs used in the matching exercise to the teacher. He also held onto the line drawings and repeatedly examined them for some time after the assessment.

Conclusions   Matu can correctly discriminate materials as abstract as line drawings, but has difficulty matching partial objects to whole objects. It is interesting to note that he performs better on the picture to object task than the identical object match. This apparent discrepancy in performance at the varying levels of abstraction may be partially explained by prior experience with and the motivating aspects of the materials used. Matu was often asked to match pictures in several daily instructional sessions and was, therefore, familiar with that activity. Additionally, it was reported that one of his favorite free-time activities was to repetitively line up and visually examine a set of picture cards, similar to those used in the matching tasks. It was noted Matu had some trouble scanning the objects but responded well to pointing as a means of assistance in scanning the materials. It appears that pictures or symbols may be appropriate for use in a communication system for Matu.

Question 3:   What Is Matu's Level of Speech and Language Use and Comprehension?

Assessments   A series of classroom observations and assessments of Matu's speech and language abilities indicated that he was capable of verbal initiations and responses. Observations were made by the CDS during a 7-day period using a data sheet developed specifically for this case. Sample data collected are contained in Figure 7.9. During these observations and assessments, the CDS recorded the number of replies of two or more words in response to open-ended questions, and the number of verbal initiations of two or more words during a two-and-a-half-hour period each day. She also recorded, verbatim, his verbalizations in each instance.

Results   The results of the observations and assessments show that Matu initiated verbal interactions more frequently than he responded to open-ended questions. During the 7 days of observation, Matu only answered three open-ended questions; however, he produced 20 verbal initiations during that same time period. Most of these verbalizations (i.e., 16) were three words or longer and were appropriate for the situation. His most typical response to the questions was to turn away or

Name:	Matu		Date:	4/20 to 4/23

Time	Open-ended questions answered (2 or more words; example)	Verbal initiations (2 or more words; example)
12:30–1:30 P.M.	Q: "What was that book about, Matu?" A: "Train drives" and then he made train noises.	"They're swinging," Matu said as he paged through a book and saw an illustration of a playground.
1:30–2:00 P.M.	Q: "Do you want to go outside?" A: "Want to go out and play on the grass."	"This is itch," pointing to finger. "This is itch." "Get me it," referring to ointment for finger.
2:30–3:10 P.M.		"Tie the shoelaces," Matu said as he stood near the teacher with untied shoes.

Figure 7.9. Data collected on verbal responses and initiations.

look away from the person asking the question. The majority of the verbal initiations were requests for objects or for action from a nearby adult (e.g., "Get me a tape," "Tie my shoe."). No initiations were directed to peers.

Conclusions Although too few observations and assessments were made to obtain an estimate of Matu's mean length of utterances, he was able to use verbalizations up to five words long, with most utterances being three words or longer. The majority of the utterances were self-initiated and he rarely responded to questions; thus, questioning was not an effective method of communicating with Matu. A more visual approach to communication was thought to be more appropriate.

Question 4: In Which Situations or Activities Did Matu Appear to be in Greatest Need of a More Formal Means to Communicate His Intents?

Assessment As was previously described, Matu used a variety of nonverbal behaviors to communicate. Most often he used these to escape from situations in which he was requested to perform tasks or when changing from one task or work area to another in the classroom. The teacher indicated that Matu had a difficult time changing tasks in situations outside of the classroom as well.

Results The results showed that, when attempting to change activities or persons, Matu would resist the attempts by running away, clinging to the materials with which he was working, or would begin to yell, scream, and tantrum. These behaviors, although seen as a means of communicating, were extremely disruptive to the others in his class and required an inordinate amount of teacher time to resolve.

Conclusions It appears that Matu needs a more formal means of communication when changing activities to allow for a smoother and more consistent flow of his daily instructional activities. His temper tantrums and running away are disruptive to his classmates and, as stated before, require quite a lot of teacher and staff time and energy.

Summary of Results Used in Selecting the System

Although capable of using some verbal language to make requests, Matu generally used a variety of nonverbal behaviors (e.g., passive gaze, running away, finger flicking) to communicate. He was able to match objects that were similar and of the same function, and also able to match photographs and line drawings to real objects. While there was no information available on his communication needs in the home, Matu had a difficult time transitioning between activities and classroom staff. When the teacher or aide led Matu to his next activity, he frequently passively resisted or ran away. Matu appeared to need a more formal system of communication to allow for smooth transitions between activities and instructional areas throughout the school day and to allow him a means of communicating with others.

Using the above information, the following systems were considered for use with Matu:

1. A purely verbal approach was considered for Matu. With such an approach, he would be expected to communicate

verbally with other peers and adults in all of his daily activities. However, this was not used because the information available at the time indicated that Matu would probably rely upon his nonverbal means of communication in the classroom. Also, attempts to "have" him speak (e.g., during speech therapy) or waiting for him to talk, met with resistance and resulted in crying, tantruming, and general classroom disruption.

2. A pictorial approach was considered for use as a communication system for Matu. With this system, he would utilize some type of communication booklet or board with pictures for the major daily classroom activities and materials. However, since Matu occasionally initiated some speech, the teacher thought that the communication cards might inhibit further speech development. Also, the communication board would inhibit his mobility to other environments.

3. The system that was ultimately used was not a communication system per se, but rather a daily classroom schedule system. Although an eventual goal was to provide a more formal method of communication for Matu, the teacher and the CDS decided that Matu should first learn to transition easily from activity to activity in the classroom. They felt that many of his behavioral outbursts could be attributed to his apparent lack of understanding of the routine involved in the classroom and to his subsequent inability to handle effectively changes from one activity to the next. In addition, through the pairing of verbalizations with the use of the schedule system, the teacher and the CDS hoped to facilitate Matu's independent verbalizations.

SYSTEM'S ACTUAL DESIGN

The CDS and the teacher devised a daily activity schedule system to assist Matu in transitions from one activity to another during the school day. The system consisted of a posterboard with a number of pockets that corresponded to the number of daily activities in the classroom. Each activity was represented by a line drawing on a 5 inch by 7 inch card. The name of the activity was printed on each card (see Figure 7.10).

The purposes of the system were to:

1. Provide opportunities for verbal and nonverbal communication regarding school activities.
2. Develop familiarity with a daily routine by using pictures of the classroom activities on a consistent basis.
3. Provide variability in Matu's daily routine at a later date by gradually introducing changes into the picture schedule by rearranging the schedule or by using new pictures for new activities.

The following general instructional objective was developed for Matu's use of the system: *Matu will use his daily schedule system independently or with verbal prompting to transition from activity to activity throughout the day.*

Each day, the teacher or classroom aide would arrange the line drawings in the pockets on the schedule in the order of the day's activities. Upon arrival in the classroom, Matu would be verbally and physically (if necessary) directed to go to the ac-

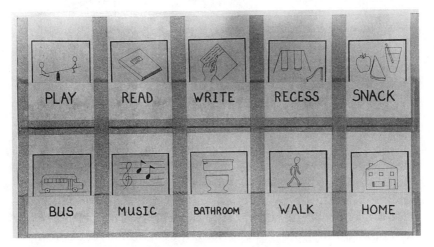

Figure 7.10. Matu's schedule system.

tivity schedule to identify the first activity. Verbal comments, such as, "It's time to get started" or, "It's time to get to work," were provided by the teacher or the aide. A least-to-most prompting system was used to facilitate the use of the system. This is explained in the previous case history of Kyle (pp. 156–157).

Before each prompt, the teacher or aide paused to allow Matu the opportunity to get the appropriate card without further prompting. The natural cues for Matu to choose the correct activity card were: entry into the classroom if he was using the system for the first time that day or end of an activity for all other card selections. If he chose the wrong card, it was placed back in the schedule and the next level of prompt was given. Once the correct card was obtained, Matu was verbally praised, asked to repeat the name of the activity, and then directed to go to the activity, taking the card with him. Upon finishing the activity, the teacher told Matu that he was finished. He was then led back to the schedule, if necessary, assisted in putting the activity card back in the appropriate pocket, and then prompted to use the schedule for the next activity.

EFFECTIVENESS OF THE SYSTEM

Data were collected by the CDS and a graduate student in special education, during two different time frames, on Matu's use of the schedule system. The system was used during school hours only. The first set of observations occurred immediately after the introduction of the system during the summer. Data were collected for $1^{1}/_{2}$ months during the academic year, during which time 64 opportunities to use the system were observed. The second set of observations occurred one year later during the following summer. For this 1 month period, 61 opportunities to use the system were observed. (It should be noted that Matu had a different teacher and was in a different classroom during the second summer observation period.) For each opportunity to use the system, the highest level of prompt used was recorded. The percentages of total observations for each level of prompt needed for correct use during both observation periods were graphed and are shown in Figure 7.11. Interrater reliability, collected during the observations, ranged from 75%–100%, with a mean of 91%.

The data indicate that Matu required less assistance during the second observation period. Anecdotal reports from the teacher and classroom aide for the first summer showed that Matu would run from the activity, throw the picture card on the floor, and frequently not engage in the activity after being prompted to use the system. Observations and data collected on Matu's behavior in the second summer showed that he engaged in the activities and behaved appropriately 80% of the time. It is possible that the improvement in Matu's behavior may have been the result of one or a combination of several factors. Certainly, he was becoming accustomed to the daily

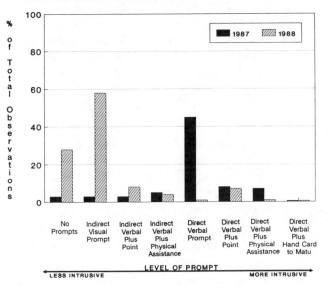

Objective: Given an indirect verbal and gestural cue, Matu will use his daily schedule system to transition from activity to activity throughout the day at least 80% of the time for 5 consecutive days.

Figure 7.11. Summary of procedural data on prompts required for Matu to use his schedule system.

classroom routine. Also, Matu was using his schedule system more independently, which may have helped to relieve his apparent anxiety about changing activities. Finally, Matu used more verbal communication the second summer and, thus, may have been more easily able to communicate his concerns to the teacher and aides. The teacher also indicated that Matu was beginning to recite the words on the cards as he picked them up and was beginning to verbally interact with the adults in the classroom more frequently.

SUMMARY

Matu made progress in the use of his schedule system, but several aspects of it could be changed. First, as noted above, this system is a *schedule system*, not a formal communication system. One suggestion would be to incorporate the salient aspects of the schedule system into a method that would allow Matu to interact more frequently and appropriately with others. This might be accomplished by utilizing a nonhandicapped partner in the transition of classroom activities. This partner could assist Matu, when necessary, in using a pictorial system to move from one activity to another. His verbal language might also be stimulated if he was required to verbally label the picture of the activity with his partner. This might then serve as an impetus for the partner to maintain an interaction with Matu.

It should be noted that Matu's schedule system was not very portable. When he went to the regular classroom or into the community for instruction, it was not feasible for him to go back to the special education classroom to change activity cards each time there was a change. One possible remedy may be to reduce the size of the cards and to place them in a wallet sized holder that Matu could carry with him. This would allow Matu to take his system with him and require him to use the system in a variety of settings. Additionally, other communication cards could then be more easily added to match the larger range of expected activities and materials that he might encounter.

Also, there was some indication from his teacher that Matu was understanding the relationship between the activity cards and the activities themselves. This was noted when he began to name the activities as he picked up the cards. It is possible that Matu might eventually be able to learn to sight read the words on the cards and that this ability should be considered, pending his progress. In addition, favorite activity cards should be placed in a communication "system" that he could carry. Matu should be offered opportunities to initiate requests for these activities using the activity cards.

Finally, Matu's system should be expanded and used at home, if his parents so desire. Again, using a picture system in another setting and with additional pictures would expand his opportunities for interactions, particularly with his family, other relatives, and children in his neighborhood.

NAME: Jodi
AGE: 11 years
TEACHER: Peggy Scuderi
COMMUNICATIONS
DISORDERS
SPECIALIST: Chris Englehart

SYSTEM

This case history describes a schedule system of concrete objects used to represent daily classroom activities for a student with severe disabilities. Questions and procedures used to determine the appropriate system are presented along with data on the student's use of the system. Suggestions for alternative systems are discussed.

OVERVIEW

Jodi lives at home with her mother, stepfather, two younger brothers, and a younger sister. Both parents work, yet they have flexible schedules that allow them to attend to Jodi's health and educational needs. Jodi was diagnosed as having severe mental retardation, autism, and Rett syndrome. Rett syndrome is a progressively degenerative condition affecting only females and is characterized by severe dementia, autism, loss of purposeful hand use, loss of or generally ataxic gait, stereotypical hand movements such as hand wringing or hand biting, and acquired microcephaly (Hagberg, Aicardi, Dias, & Ramos, 1983). Jodi received special education and related services in a self-contained special education classroom in a public elementary school. A classroom aide assisted her in all classroom activities.

INFORMATION FROM SCHOOL RECORDS

The information that follows includes Jodi's status from the school records on cognition, motor skills, vision and hearing, medical, communication skills, speech and language, parent concerns, and social/interpersonal behavior.

179

Cognition

The Peabody Picture Vocabulary Test (PPVT) (Dunn, 1965) was administered for an estimate of Jodi's cognitive and communicative abilities. Her raw score on the test was a 2 and no scaled score could be determined. Shortly prior to the current school year, a developmental assessment was completed at a medical facility. The report indicated that she had "severe developmental delay in all areas." Her estimated cognitive abilities were at the 12–18 month level, as she would perform skills such as handing a tape player to an adult in order to have it turned on, using a common object in a functional manner (e.g., washes her face with a washcloth), and anticipating lunch by going to the classroom door when told that it is lunchtime.

Motor Skills

Jodi has moderate spasticity in her legs and receives physical therapy. She has poor balance when walking, requiring assistance to travel more than 10 feet, and when negotiating steps or uneven surfaces. Jodi has fine motor problems that result in a weak grasp and poor control of her fingers. She utilizes a gross radial palmar grasp and is unable to pick up small objects neatly. Both her fine motor and gross motor skills are characteristic of children with Rett's syndrome.

Vision and Hearing

There were no vision or hearing reports on file. Her teacher reported, however, that Jodi does not consistently maintain eye contact with persons or the tasks on which she is working, and does not always respond to verbal requests or to her name.

Medical

Jodi was diagnosed as having nocturnal (i.e., nighttime) seizures at the age of 7 and began having right side tonic seizures when she was 8. She is taking Tegretol and Depakene to control the seizures. Additionally, Jodi is especially sensitive to colds and the flu and absent many days from school due to these illnesses.

Communication Skills

Jodi said her first words (i.e., mama, dada, no) at approximately 18 months of age. However, by the time she was 3 years old, she was no longer speaking, a typical outcome of children with Rett syndrome. At 20 months, she began to continually wring her hands and chew on them. While she continues to exhibit these behaviors, verbal cues such as "hands down" or "hands quiet" cause her to cease for a few minutes. Instruction in sign language had occurred for approximately 3 years; however, Jodi was still unable to use signs without physical assistance. Her mother reported that the family understood Jodi's moods and actions well enough to communicate with her at home. For example, when Jodi would stand near the kitchen sink, the family members knew that Jodi wanted a drink of water.

Speech and Language

Two instruments were used to assess Jodi's speech and language abilities at school. As mentioned above, Jodi received credit for only two items on the PPVT. Although she received no scaled score on the test, she did attempt to respond to the test items by pointing to the pictures when prompted. The communication subsection of the TARC assessment system (Sailor & Mix, 1975) was also administered. She received credit for 34% of the possible items including the following skills: follows some directions, uses a few understandable words (rarely), obeys the commands of "no" or "stop that," responds to her name by eye contact, points to objects or people when requested, responds to and enjoys music, and follows simple one-step directions. Presently, Jodi may say a word, or even a complete sentence, but it is usually inappropriate in the context and appears unrelated to any external cues. Most verbalizations are characterized as unintelligible "jibberish." Jodi does not imitate sounds, but may say "dada" or "mama," non-specifically. Overall, her speech and language skills appear to be at the 8–12-month level.

Parent Concerns

A parent interview was completed to obtain information about Jodi's preferences for objects and activities, and to discuss parent priorities and long-term goals for her. Jodi's mother indicated that Jodi enjoyed having books read to her, listening to music, watching television, going for car rides, and being around other people. She listed toileting skills, communication, physical stamina, and independent eating as parent priorities for Jodi. The following long-term goals were developed by the teacher and Jodi's mother:

1. To tell someone when she has to use the bathroom
2. To eliminate in the toilet
3. To communicate her needs to others
4. To walk up and down inclines independently
5. To eat independently using utensils and linen
6. To turn on a water faucet, fill a glass, and turn off the faucet independently
7. To sit in a chair and pay attention to one person for 2 minutes
8. To walk up and down stairs independently
9. To put on or take off her coat

Social/Interpersonal Behavior

Jodi was noted to enjoy being in close proximity with other students and adults. She frequently attempted to maintain peer-initiated contacts by smiling at the peer, touching him or her, and making appropriate eye contact. Although she could not easily follow peers at recess because of her mobility problems, she would continue to watch them play while they were nearby. The Adaptive Behavior Evaluation Scale (ABES) (Mc-Carney, 1983) was administered to Jodi when she was 10 years old. She received the following subsection scale scores (the mean = 10; standard deviation = 3):

Environmental-interpersonal behaviors	0
Self-related behavior	0
Task-related behavior	0
Total adaptive behavior quotient	0

The test report indicated that Jodi needed physical assistance in all interpersonal behaviors such as displaying appropriate behavior in group settings, accepting changes in routines, and interacting appropriately with peers and adults in school and nonschool situations.

ASSESSMENT FOR COMMUNICATION SYSTEM PLANNING

The teacher and the Communications Disorders Specialist (CDS) had considered using a communication or schedule system comprised of real objects with Jodi because of her level of functioning and her limited conceptual abilities. The following assessments were, thus, used to help determine the format and organization of a system. In particular, information was needed on Jodi's visual tracking, eye-hand coordination, and matching abilities, along with an analysis of her pragmatic communicative intents. Examples of data collected are included for some assessment areas.

Question 1: What Are Jodi's Visual Tracking and Scanning Abilities?

Although medical reports indicated that Jodi had no apparent visual deficits, there was some concern that she might be unable to track or visually locate objects in some visual fields. Knowledge of Jodi's visual tracking and scanning abilities would allow the teacher to know where to present objects or pictures and gestures/signs during communication training. For example, if it was shown that she could not see objects to her far right, the teacher would be careful not to put anything to that side if she wanted Jodi to see it.

Assessment   The assessment was conducted using two items that the teacher reported that Jodi liked, namely crackers and a storybook. Each item was held at Jodi's eye level, approximately 18 inches away and moved in various directions.

Results   Jodi successfully tracked all objects horizontally, vertically, and diagonally with a smooth, continuous motion as long as the objects were at or below her eye level. When the objects were moved above eye level, she did not visually locate or track them.

Conclusion   Jodi exhibited good head posture (i.e., steady and aligned) and showed no signs of nystagmus (i.e., bouncing eyes) or strabismus (i.e., eyes turning in or out) during the assessment.

Question 2:   What Are Jodi's Eye-Hand Coordination Abilities?

Assessment   Jodi's eye-hand coordination was informally assessed in the classroom. This was necessitated by her fine motor difficulties. Also, the teacher and CDS were contemplating using real objects for a system, and they were concerned about her ability to manipulate the objects. The assessment was completed once with Jodi sitting, and again when she was standing.

Results   The assessment was done for both the sitting and standing positions because the teacher and CDS were concerned about her stability and mobility while manipulating objects. When standing, Jodi could directly reach for and grasp objects up to 18 inches away from her to the front and to both sides. However, she could not grasp objects that were more than 18 inches away from her. Jodi primarily used her left hand for reaching and grasping, and was able to cross midline to get objects. When sitting, she reached for objects in all directions and could obtain items 18 inches away or further by leaning toward the object. Again, she used her left hand and was able to cross midline. Jodi was unable to pick up objects from the floor, from either a sitting or standing position, without considerable physical assistance for balance and support.

Conclusion Jodi primarily used her left hand for reaching and grasping objects, and was able to cross midline to get objects at various distances depending on her position (e.g., standing, sitting).

Question 3: What Are Jodi's Matching/Discrimination Abilities?

Assessment The teacher observed that when a common functional object (e.g., book, shoe, cup) was named and placed in front of Jodi, that Jodi would pick it up; however, this could only be done when there were no other objects or distractions in front of Jodi. For example, when presented with a place setting of a cup, spoon, and plate, Jodi would hand the object to the teacher upon command.

Results In an informal matching exercise, Jodi correctly matched one object to one of two other functional objects with only 33% accuracy. For example, during one matching trial, Jodi was presented with a book and a cup, shown another cup by the teacher, and asked to find one like it. Jodi incorrectly picked up the book and held it out to the teacher.

Conclusion The teacher reported that she frequently had to physically turn Jodi's head toward the task and that she felt that Jodi did not completely comprehend the task. For this reason, no other more complicated matching or discrimination tasks (e.g., using line drawings or photographs) were attempted.

Question 4: What Behaviors Does Jodi Use to Communicate, and What Intents Are Expressed?

Assessment During a 2-month period, Jodi was observed interacting with teachers, peers, and other classroom staff. These interactions included responding to teacher or staff requests, initiating and maintaining personal contact with peers and others, entering and leaving the classroom, and participating in a large number of group and one-to-one instructional activities.

Results The pragmatic intents of her interactions were recorded and coded into one of seven categories adapted from Dore (1974, 1975). The categories included giving an answer, expressing emotions, engaging in interpersonal contact, making a request, describing an event or object, entertaining or teasing, and other. The data collection process involved observing 120 interactions during a 2-month period. For each interaction, the rater (a graduate student in special education) recorded the approximate time and location of the interaction, made a check mark in the appropriate category on the rating form, and wrote a brief description that included an interpretation of the intent of the interaction. Figure 7.12 contains a sample data sheet completed for one observation period (see Appendix A.8 for a blank Pragmatic Intent Observation Data sheet).

A second rater was present during approximately 15% of the interactions and coded them using the same coding system. Interrater reliability on the coding of the interactions during these simultaneous observations was 100%. The data indicate that more than half (52%) of Jodi's social interactions in the classroom were in response to a staff member or teacher's request to perform some action or movement (e.g., sit down, come here). Approximately 43% of her interactions were to express her emotions and feelings to others via smiles or laughing, or to initiate or maintain interpersonal contact with others by touching them on the arm or maintaining eye contact.

Conclusion These results show that Jodi could and would nonverbally communicate with others in the classroom.

Summary of Results Used in Selecting a System

The results of the assessments that were used to answer the preceding questions show that Jodi had adequate visual tracking skills, except above eye level; used her left hand to reach and grasp objects; could pick up a familiar object when it was named and when few distractors were present; and used a

Pragmatic Intent Observation Data

Name: _____ Jodi _____   Date: _____ 11/17/89 _____   Observer: _____ B.A. _____

Categories	Location/time/frequency	Example of activity and interpretation (write up third example observed)	Other comments
1. Makes a request; asks a question			
2. Gives an answer or responds to a question or request	8:45 A.M.—toileting three times 9:00 A.M.—small group seven times	Followed aide to bathroom upon request. Responded to "sit down," "look at book," and others	
3. Describes events or aspects of the environment			
4. Expresses facts, beliefs, attitudes, or emotions	8:30 A.M.—entering room twice	Smiled and looked at Gretchen when she said hello. Started to giggle when she saw the teacher.	
5. Attempts to and does establish or maintain interpersonal contact or interaction	9:00 A.M.—small group activity four times	Touched aide's arm when she looked away from Jodi. Kept eye contact with peer and smiled intermittently at peer.	
6. Attempts to entertain or tease others			

Figure 7.12. Sample of pragmatic intent observation data for Jodi.

variety of nonverbal means to communicate in the classroom. The implications for developing a communication system would include: using concrete objects that are familiar to Jodi to facilitate conceptual understanding, placing objects at or below eye level to make sure she sees them, making sure the objects are within easy reach, and allowing her opportunities to not only respond to others, but to initiate interactions with them. Additionally, by presenting two or three objects to Jodi and allowing her free choice of objects, Jodi would have greater opportunity to choose the activities in which she wanted to participate.

SYSTEM'S ACTUAL DESIGN

A daily schedule system utilizing a series of concrete (i.e., real object) representations of school activities was developed by Jodi's teacher and the CDS. The teacher and the CDS thought that Jodi needed an established routine on which to base her future communicative interactions. Thus, a schedule system rather than a communication system, per se, was used. The rationale behind this decision was that Jodi needed consistent activities to which she could relate the real objects that were used to represent those events. The decision to use real objects was based upon the finding that Jodi's conceptual abilities were limited, and, thus, she may be unable to effectively match more abstract communication symbols with the activities. The objects used in the schedule (e.g., toilet paper roll for toileting, a purse for community shopping, a cup for snack) were placed in a row of small cardboard boxes on a countertop in the classroom. Figure 7.13 contains a picture of the system. The long-term goal of the teacher was gradually to fade out the real objects and to introduce photographs of activities or objects so that Jodi could use a more portable communication board or booklet. The short-term objectives for Jodi's use of the system were as follows:

1. Teach Jodi to become accustomed to daily classroom routines.

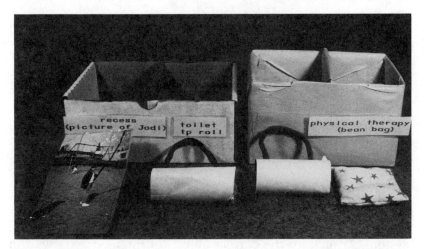

Figure 7.13. Jodi's schedule system. Handles on toilet paper roll help Jodi to hold them.

2. Teach Jodi to initiate interactions in the classroom.

These short-term objectives were seen as necessary precursors to Jodi's use of an object system to communicate intents. For example, once Jodi became familiar with an established classroom schedule, the teacher could then allow Jodi an opportunity to independently initiate activities by presenting the schedule object to the teacher or aide. In essence, the schedule of activities would become a focal point of interaction for Jodi.

Jodi was verbally and physically prompted to go to the boxes, to pick up the appropriate object for the activity, and to proceed to the activity. When the activity was completed, she returned to the boxes, replaced the object, and picked up the object for the next activity. A least-to-most prompting system was used by the teacher or classroom staff to assist Jodi's use of the schedule. The levels of prompts were: 1) independent performance—no prompts; 2) verbal prompt—"Jodi, pick up the _____;" 3) gestural prompt—point to the appropriate object; 4) physical orientation of her head to the task; and 5) complete physical assistance—hand over hand.

EFFECTIVENESS OF THE SYSTEM

Data were collected on Jodi's use of the system during a 2-month period. Because of illnesses and the accompanying absences from school, only eight observations were completed. A classroom aide, however, indicated that Jodi's use of the system during those observations was typical of her daily ability. As an additional note, Jodi was also undergoing a change in her seizure medication during the observation period, frequently had seizures, and was reportedly groggy during school.

During the observations, each time Jodi used her system, an observer recorded the level of prompting required for her to perform each step of system use. The steps were: 1) go to the system, 2) pick up the correct object for the next activity, and 3) go to the activity. Figure 7.14 (see Appendix A.10 for a blank form) shows sample data on the prompts needed for Jodi to use

Form for Collecting Procedural Data on Use of a System

Name: _____Jodi_____   Date: __12–9–88__

Observer: _____B.A._____   Time of day: ___A.M./P.M.___

System activity	Goes to system	Gets object/symbol	Goes to activity
1. Toileting	P	V	P
2. Matching exercise	P	OH	P
3. Reading group	P	I	V
4. Recess	P	OH	V
5. Physical therapy	P	P	P
6. Toileting	V	OH	P
7. Lunch	V	I	V

Key: I = Independent; V = Verbal prompt; G = Gestural prompt; OH = Orients head; P = Physical assistance.

Comments:

Figure 7.14. Sample data on prompts used by Jodi.

her system. For three observation sessions, a second observer recorded data on the level of prompting required. Interrater reliability ranged from 83%–100%, with a mean of 92%.

One goal was for Jodi to perform the steps involved in using the system either independently or with verbal prompting. Her performance for each observation session was summarized in terms of the percentage of steps completed independently or with verbal prompting for all opportunities to use the system. A graph of Jodi's progress is contained in Figure 7.15. The data show that Jodi's use of the system was at best erratic and unpredictable. The percentage of steps completed with no prompts or with verbal prompts ranged from 8%–78%, with a mean of 32%. On only two occasions was the percentage of steps completed above 33%. Jodi's poor performance could be due to her illnesses and absences from school or to physiological fluctuations resulting from changes in her medication. Also, although data were collected as frequently as possible, the lack of daily data collection may not give a true picture of Jodi's ability to use the system. However, as mentioned previously, a classroom aide noted that Jodi's performance during the observation session was typical of her overall ability to use the system.

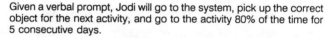

Instructional Goal: Given a verbal prompt, Jodi will go to the system, pick up the correct object for the next activity, and go to the activity 80% of the time for 5 consecutive days.

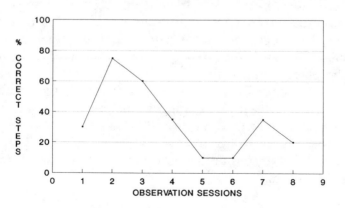

Figure 7.15.   Summary of data on Jodi's use of her schedule system.

Shortly after the last observation, Jodi became very ill and missed nearly three consecutive weeks of school. Upon return she was even more motorically unstable and even refused to walk at times. At this time, the CDS and the classroom teacher decided to discontinue use of the system until Jodi's health and mobility improved.

SUMMARY

This case study illustrates some problems that are commonly encountered when developing communication systems for persons with severe disabilities. Behavioral and physiological fluctuations due to seizures and illness and frequent absences complicate efforts to develop effective communication systems. In Jodi's case, several alternatives are apparent. First, her current system of concrete representations of daily classroom activities could be continued with the hope that her mobility and health difficulties would improve; however, the general prognosis for children with Rett syndrome is for gradual and progressive loss of ability. Perhaps a more practical and functional approach would be to try to expand and refine Jodi's present nonverbal means of communication (e.g., smiles, eye contact, touches). This would be advantageous as her mobility problems would not interfere greatly with using these gestures. In addition, most people who have regular contact with Jodi can already discern her communicative intents through these means. This approach would require that people who are unfamiliar with Jodi (e.g., new bus drivers, some of the students on the playground) receive instruction in her communication forms. It is generally best if one person is in charge of training these people. While these suggestions are not the only possibilities available or appropriate for alternative systems for Jodi, they do illustrate the ways in which her teacher could further examine communication options for students with severe disabilities.

CHAPTER
EIGHT

Factors Salient in Systems Used by Adolescents and Adults

The factors mentioned previously in Chapters Six and Seven are equally pertinent when considering systems for adolescents and adults. However, the significance of age, remaining years of educational services, preferences of caregivers/parents, and the emphasis on interactions are weighted quite differently. For adolescents and adults, the phrase, "The time has come," seems appropriate. These individuals have been in learning and nurturing environments directed toward preparing them for the transition to a work- and community-centered life. The emphasis for persons in this age group is upon using their skills and abilities more than it is upon learning new ones. Thus, systems designed for persons who will be leaving educational services shortly, or who have already left, should reflect this work- and community-centered life. The case histories that follow illustrate some of the differences in system selection that result from this orientation.

The first case history in this chapter is about Jesse, who was still in high school and had one remaining year in which to develop a communication system. His school program involved community instruction in a number of nonschool environments, although it was limited because of his behavior. It was important that the system work both in school and in community environments, and that it not stigmatize him by drawing attention to his lack of speech and his mental disability. At the same time, there was both time and resources to start on an initial system and to expand to another system since his behavior was viewed as communicative and his interactions became more consistent.

The case history of Ernie illustrates a similar approach in viewing his problem behaviors as communicative. However, his age was a significant factor in the selection of a system that was as close to a formal system as feasible and as readily understood by familiar and unfamiliar people as possible. The result was a system that enabled Ernie to interact; however, he could select messages only with assistance. Thus, although Ernie did benefit from his communication system through increased interactions in many environments, he remained dependent upon others to use it. This was seen as the most viable option that appeared to be consistent with the philosophic assumptions and practical considerations that are discussed in Chapter One and the reality of his age, his time-limited consultation remaining, and the decreased number of personnel with minimal education background that could assist Ernie in expanding his system.

JESSE

NAME: Jesse
AGE: 19 years
TEACHER: Margaret
               Baldwin
CONSULTANT: Edwin
               Helmstetter

SYSTEM

Jesse's system resulted when his communication partners viewed his problem behaviors as attempts to communicate rather than as just problem behaviors. The communicative functions of the behaviors were assessed and Jesse was taught to use other more appropriate responses in his behavioral repertoire as a means of communication.

OVERVIEW AND INFORMATION FROM SCHOOL RECORDS

The following is an overview and information from Jesse's school records that included his diagnosis, reason for referral, history of development, educational performance, educational program description, and behavioral interventions.

Diagnosis

School records indicated that Jesse "had autistic-like features" and demonstrated a "refusal to relate to others verbally." Although school records reported that his IQ was 22, his teacher questioned the accuracy of the report. Following intervention, Jesse's behavior changed significantly. Although he was not reassessed for diagnostic purposes, his teacher suspected that he had been emotionally disturbed and electively mute.

Reason for Referral

Jesse screamed approximately five times a day. The average duration of each episode of screaming was 25 minutes, al-

---

This case history has been co-authored by Margaret Baldwin (first author), Teacher, Wenatchee School District, Wenatchee, Washington.

though episodes could continue for as long as 3 hours. His screams were loud, continuous vocalizations with only momentary pauses to catch his breath. Jesse would also run and jump about the room while he screamed, and would hit anyone who was in his path or bang and destroy property. Occasionally, he would abuse himself by banging his head on walls, or slapping and scratching his face. Unless interrupted, the self-injury would continue for up to $1^1/_2$ minutes.

History of Development

Very little of Jesse's early developmental history was evident in his school records. While planning an intervention for his problem behaviors, however, the following information was obtained from his family and physician.

Jesse developed normally until age 4, at which time his family moved to a new area of the country. His parents reported that during the transition, he began to tantrum and scream, stopping only to sleep. He also became severely withdrawn. About that time, the family's physician suggested that Jesse had autism and should be placed out of the home. By 6 years of age, he was residing in a group home and attending a special school for students with moderate mental retardation. His skills continued to deteriorate and, at 8 years of age, he was placed in a classroom for students with severe disabilities. He also began taking a psychotropic medication to control his self-abuse and aggression. At 14 years of age, he began having seizures, and an antiepileptic drug was added to his medical regimen. He continued on both the psychotropic and anti-epileptic medications, as well as medication for his complexion, throughout the course of the present intervention.

Educational Performance

Based upon the results of the Vineland Adaptive Behavior Scale (VABS) (Sparrow, Balla, & Cicchetti, 1984) and the Developmental Profile II (Alpern, Boll, & Shearer, 1984), Jesse's receptive language was at the level of responding to three-part commands; however, he had very little expressive communication. As was learned later, however, screams, aggression, and self-injury could have represented Jesse's communicative intents.

In terms of self-help skills, Jesse could properly use eating utensils, although he ate very rapidly. He was independent at toileting, except for the use of toilet paper. He could dress himself when provided with verbal instructions, except for tying shoes. He was unable to shower or shave himself. Jesse's gross and fine motor skills were well developed; however, he did walk with a stiff-legged gait and had difficulty supinating his hands and arms, such as when he needed to carry objects. In addition to the behavioral problems described earlier, Jesse also became aggressive when he was touched, and would slap, kick, and butt the individual with his head, as well as scream.

Educational Program Description

Jesse was in a public high school, special education classroom for students with severe learning and behavioral problems. The program, which emphasized the preparation of students to be able to live and work in community settings, involved a significant amount of instruction at job sites, restaurants, stores, and other off-campus locations. However, because of Jesse's behavior, his teacher had greatly curtailed his off-campus programs. He would sometimes scream the entire time that he was in a store and deliberately knock merchandise off of display tables.

At school, Jesse's instruction focused upon personal management, social adjustment, personal safety, and vocational skills training. Nondisabled peers were his companions and tutors at school and during community instruction. His screams, however, which were audible throughout the school, disrupted other students' programs.

In terms of support services, Jesse began receiving speech and language services when he was 4 years old. Instruction included producing sounds, naming objects and pictures, sign language, and using picture cards to communicate. At the time of this intervention, his receptive communication skills were excellent. He could comply with commands, such as, "Get a spoon," and, "Get ready, it's time to go shopping." In terms of expressive communication, however, no means had been found that Jesse used to make his needs known. In fact, because of his history of failure with therapy, he was no longer receiving speech and language services from a communication disorder specialist (CDS). His individualized education program (IEP), however, did include communication objectives that were implemented by his teachers. These included the use of sign language, gestures, pictures, and vocalizations to request objects and persons and to express other needs related to his daily activities (e.g., vocational instruction, lunch, community travel).

Behavioral Interventions

Several behavioral interventions had been used in order to reduce Jesse's screaming, self-abuse, and aggression. The interventions included ignoring the behaviors, placing him in a time-out room until he stopped screaming or abusing himself, and restraining his hands whenever he became self-abusive or aggressive toward other persons. Another program involved reinforcing him for maintaining relatively quiet intervals of time with two items that he greatly enjoyed—drinks of water and face cream. This program was effective in that it created momentary periods of quiet. However, he still screamed an average of four to five times each school day. Furthermore, he made little educational progress, preferring instead to withdraw for long periods of time under a table. In the classroom, his only form of interaction with others was through screaming and aggression.

ASSESSMENT FOR
COMMUNICATION SYSTEM PLANNING

The teacher decided to regard Jesse's problem behaviors of screaming, running from the room, holding his face in his hands, being aggressive, rubbing lotion on his face, and inflicting self-injury as attempts to communicate. Without additional information, however, it was impossible to ascertain Jesse's level of intent (e.g., were the behaviors emotional outbursts, did he have a plan that was goal directed) or the specific goals, if any, that he had in mind (e.g., escape). It was necessary, therefore, to establish whether the behaviors were associated with specific events, in which case it might be possible to teach Jesse to substitute more acceptable behaviors to serve the same function.

The following series of questions and procedures, as described in Chapter Two, summarizes the process of assessing behavior in preparation for implementing communication skill training as an alternative to focusing only upon problem behavior.

Question 1: What Occurred Before, During, and After the Problem Behaviors?

The classroom staff observed Jesse and maintained a written record each time a behavior occurred. They noted the form of the behavior (e.g., screaming, running from the room, slapping his own face), what happened as a consequence (e.g., teacher ignored the behavior, peer moved away from him), and what he did next. One pattern that emerged was that Jesse would hold his face and begin rocking. This was usually ignored. After a short time, he would begin to scream. A second pattern was one that began with Jesse screaming, followed by running from the room, usually to the water fountain for a drink. On his way to the fountain, he aggressed toward anyone who interfered with him. A third pattern was identified while he rode the bus or van between the school and community sites. Jesse's screams were punctuated by hitting the vehicle's windows, on some instances with enough force to shatter them. The fourth pattern involved Jesse suddenly jumping up and hitting nearby persons or objects. If this behavior was ignored, Jesse typically exited the room and proceeded to the cafeteria to take food. Occasionally, he used the restroom, instead.

Question 2: What Were the Goals (Functions) of Jesse's Behavior?

The anecdotal information seemed to indicate that the behaviors were associated with specific events. For example, screaming and running from the room were usually associated with going to the water fountain, cafeteria, or bathroom. The purpose of these behaviors, then, would be to request objects (e.g., water, food) and actions (e.g., go to the bathroom), or to request permission (e.g., to use the bathroom).

In addition to conducting a narrative recording, the teacher reviewed Jesse's school records and contacted his family and physician in order to identify possible causes of the screaming. While no direct cause was identified, it was learned that his medications could cause insatiable thirst and dry mouth, which might explain his craving for water. In addition, the medications could cause his skin to flush or become irritated. This could explain his behavior of smearing lotion on his face. This behavior did not occur during the observation, probably because the lotion remained locked in a cabinet. As noted earlier, one of the problem behaviors was to hold his face, rock, and eventually scream. This behavior could represent discomfort due to skin irritation, and may function as a request for lotion that might soothe his skin.

If it wasn't for the fact that a solution was needed as soon as possible because the behaviors were intruding upon Jesse's education and that of other students in the school and community, it might have been possible to experimentally verify the hypotheses. For example, rate and duration of screams could have been compared across two conditions. In one condition, lasting for several days, the consequence for screams could have been permission to leave the room, but not get a drink of water. In a second condition, lasting several days, he could have been permitted to leave the room and get a drink. If the screams were associated with drinks of water, then it would be expected that the duration of each scream would be less under the second condition, although the frequency of screams might increase or remain unchanged.

Question 3: What Was
Jesse's Level of Intentionality?

There appeared little doubt that Jesse's intentionality was well-developed. He consistently used a range of different behaviors for specific purposes, so it was evident that he had goals, as well as plans, for attaining them. He also appeared able to coordinate these plans, exemplified by screaming, then waiting for a response. Furthermore, he appeared to use repair strategies (i.e., if at first he was unsuccessful, he used a different behavior, usually one more directly aimed at attaining his goal). For example, if jumping up and hitting others was ineffective, then he ran from the room and went to the cafeteria or bathroom.

Question 4: What Was
Jesse's Level of Functioning
in the Areas of Cognition, Attention,
Receptive and Expressive Communication,
Hearing and Vision, and Fine Motor Abilities?

In terms of cognitive development, Jesse demonstrated the functional use of objects, object permanence, and basic problem solving. This could indicate his readiness for a symbolic communication system. As for his attention span, Jesse could attend to instructional tasks for several minutes. However, he frequently refused to be cooperative, this being a potential barrier to enhancing his communication skills. His receptive communication appeared to be well-developed in that he could respond to three-step commands. However, he appeared unable to perform some basic receptive communication tasks such as pointing to pictures upon request. This could have represented noncompliance or a visual-perceptual problem. No visual problems were evident to the educational staff, and an ophthalmological evaluation had concluded he had normal vision.

Jesse's expressive communication abilities were described earlier (under Question 1). In addition, he made several different vocalizations. The classroom staff recorded these vocalizations and made a list of 17 sounds (e.g., "Gi go gi go, do," "barah," "bay"). It should be noted that prior to the analysis of his problem behaviors, Jesse was considered as having no form of expressive communication.

Jesse's fine motor skills were well-developed, and so this would not be an issue in the case of a manual communication system. He had no visual or auditory impairments. He could visually attend to, follow, and identify details of objects. He could locate and identify environmental sounds, and respond to commands.

Question 5: What Were Jesse's Communication Needs at Home, School, and in the Community?

Jesse lived in a group home with other individuals with disabilities. The group home staff's major concern was to eliminate Jesse's screaming, inflicting self-abuse, being aggressive, smearing lotion on his face, and drinking copious amounts of water. Receptive communication needs in the group home included compliance to staff requests. Expressive communication needs in the group home included the capability to express needs, make choices, and socialize with peers. Jesse's primary communication partners were staff and other residents at the home.

At school and in the community, Jesse's receptive communication needs related to compliance to requests that were related to safety (e.g., "walk on the sidewalk," "stop") and the learning of new tasks. The number one priority for expressive communication at school and in the community was for Jesse to state his needs or requests (e.g., water, food, bathroom) in an appropriate way. Secondary priorities included social skills, such as acknowledging the presence of others (i.e., by greeting them). His primary communication partners at school were adult staff and peers who were either nondisabled or disabled.

In the community, Jesse's communication partners included employees of restaurants and stores, school staff, and non-disabled peers who assisted with the community-based training program.

Question 6: What Means of Augmentative Communication Was Preferred by Jesse, His Family, and the Group Home Staff?

Jesse's family preferred that he learn to use sign language or pictures to communicate. The group home had tried a picture communication board, but it was unsuccessful. Jesse preferred to rip, eat, or throw the pictures, rather than use them to communicate. A sturdier communication board in which the pictures were under a plexiglass cover might have been tried, but there was a danger that he would throw the board. Furthermore, he appeared to prefer to communicate through vocalizations and motor responses. In fact, his habilitation plan at the group home included a communication-related objective that involved a motor response. When two activities were offered, Jesse indicated his selection by engaging in one of the activities.

Question 7: Which Communication System Could Be Supported by Persons in the School, Home, and Community?

Because of Jesse's preference for motor-vocal responses and his reluctance to use pictorial systems, it was decided that the search for a communication system would begin with a gestural or sign language system, combined with vocalizations. A major question then, was whether the school staff, students, and community individuals could support such a system, especially because new people often find it difficult to read gestures and signs. Fortunately, the school administration was supportive of Jesse's teacher, M. Baldwin, and made it possible for her to explain Jesse's behavior to school staff and students and to provide information about responding to his screams and related problem behaviors. Given the fact that Jesse's behavior was already an expressed concern of many of the school staff, they were more than willing to help alter this behavior. As his communication system evolved, Baldwin was able to teach the gestures and signs to those with whom Jesse frequently interacted at school. Also, because the community was small and Jesse consistently interacted with the same individuals, it was possible to instruct these people to interpret his gestures and signs.

Although a gestural/sign system could be implemented, it was hoped that Jesse would eventually cooperate in utilizing pictures as either his primary or backup system of communication. A picture system would help him reach a greater number of environments and lessen his dependence on an "interpreter" or someone to teach his system to community persons.

The group home was provided weekly written updates on Jesse's program. However, the school's educational program and the residential habilitation plans were not fully coordinated, so there was no assurance of carry over between the two agencies.

INTERVENTION

The intervention for Jesse's expressive communication system was broken down into three phases of concentration: the initial training, vocalizations and modification of gestures, and expanding his system.

Initial Training

Gestures were selected as the initial expressive communication system for Jesse to use in requesting water, lotion, and bathroom. Some of his existing motor responses were used as gestures. Whenever Jesse touched his cheek with his hands or made a similar gesture, this was interpreted as a request for lotion; when he touched himself in the genital area, this was interpreted as a request to go to the bathroom; and when he placed his hand on his mouth, he was permitted to get a drink of water.

Part of the initial instruction involved 30-minute-long one-to-one sessions on a vocational task that Jesse could successfully perform. There were two sessions each day with the classroom teacher. Pointing and modeling were used as cues for Jesse to engage in the task. He was provided with verbal and physical reinforcement for participating in the task. Self-abuse was interrupted and he was prompted to return to the task. Aggression was ignored, unless it was potentially injurious. Anytime he made a gesture that approximated touching his cheek, mouth, or genital area, he was given lotion, water, or bathroom, respectively. Initially, his daily water consumption was as much as 80 ounces. Whenever he screamed, he was provided the option of water or lotion, which he could obtain by gesturing, pointing, or reaching.

During the remainder of the school day, when Jesse screamed, he was approached and asked, verbally and with gestures, what he wanted (e.g., lotion, water, bathroom). If he approximated one of the gestures, he was provided with the object or action. If he did not gesture or continued to scream, he was verbally informed that he could get a drink or lotion, or go to the bathroom. He had free access to these, so anytime he wanted, whether or not he screamed or communicated in some other way, he could obtain water or lotion, or go to the bathroom. On these occasions, immediately after he obtained his drink or lotion, or went to the bathroom, a staff person would model the appropriate gesture.

Two weeks after the instruction began, Jesse's outbursts occurred an average of five times a day, with a mean duration of 9 minutes. This compares to the baseline rate of five times a day, with a mean duration of 25 minutes, and a maximum duration of 3 hours. His self-abuse and aggression decreased to a rate of three times a day during school hours, with a mean duration of 5 seconds. This compares to the baseline rate of 15 times a day, with a mean duration of 15 seconds, and a maximum length of 1 1/2 minutes.

Vocalizations and Modification of Gestures

The next training phase required that Jesse vocalize and use gestures that approximated American Sign Language. Whenever he requested water by placing his hand near his mouth, his request was acknowledged by, "Yes, you can have a drink of water." At the water fountain, following his drink, he was prompted to vocalize "water" and to sign "drink." He was praised for approximating the requested vocalization and gesture. There was no consequence for failure to respond. If he performed an incorrect response, the correct response was modeled again. After 10 days of instruction (i.e., 4 weeks after initial training began), he was initiating requests for water 10–12 times a day by vocalizing "wah," and approximating the sign for "drink."

As Jesse's communication improved, other staff and non-disabled peers at school were taught how to interpret and respond to his screams, gestures, and vocalizations. Also, his time in the community was increased so that he could learn to communicate with school personnel while he was in other settings, as well as with persons in the community (e.g., sign and vocalize "drink" when he was in a restaurant).

Expanding Jesse's System

New gestures and sounds were selected by analyzing those times during the day when he was most vocal and assigning gestures and sounds to specific objects and/or persons related to the ongoing activity. For example, he was quite vocal when taking a shower. Some key terms used during that activity were shower, water, and soap. The vocalizations that were assigned to these terms were "bath" (shower), "wa wa" (water), and "ssssoh" (soap). When he vocalized one of these terms, he was provided the object and prompted to produce the word and the sign. After 6 additional weeks (i.e., 10th overall week of instruction), Jesse consistently used 17 sounds and signs in the appropriate context to request objects or persons.

EFFECTIVENESS OF THE SYSTEM

After 24 weeks of instruction, Jesse appropriately initiated the use of 43 vocalization-sign/gesture combinations to communicate his needs at school and in the community. Additional examples of his vocalizations are, "Ha gi-go gi-go" accompanied by holding his hand in the air (i.e., "Hi, Peggy"), "cop-co" (i.e., popcorn), "oh" (i.e., coat), "aaht" (i.e., hat), "vvvvv" (i.e., van), and "yonyung" (i.e., hamburger).

His screaming decreased further to an average of four times a week, with a mean duration of 20 seconds. Generally, these episodes occurred when his communication partner was unsuccessful in interpreting his vocalizations and gestures. His water consumption averaged 30–40 ounces a day, an amount not considered to be excessive. The group home staff chose not to adopt this approach to communication. Instead, they continued their program to reduce his screams by providing drinks of water contingent upon periods of quiet. Unfortunately, his screaming, aggression, and self-abuse continued at the group home.

After 14 weeks of instruction, a psychologist who could interpret Jesse's gestures and vocalizations assessed his development using the VABS (Sparrow et al., 1984) and the Developmental Profile II (Alpern et al., 1984). According to the results, Jesse was at the 12–13-year level on the gross and fine motor scale, and at the 6-year level on the language scale.

Jesse also developed in other ways. He began to indicate preferences for people and places. He began to learn and to perform tasks that he had formerly resisted. For example, he began to clean tables independently, to participate in physical education class, to shower himself independently, and to assemble three-dimensional puzzles as a leisure task. He began to make eye contact when communicating and to show affection by hugging. Previously, he could not tolerate being touched. Jesse also learned to whistle and began to smile and make friends with nondisabled peers who communicated with him. He also began to "hang out" with these peers during lunch.

SUMMARY

The progress with Jesse occurred at the end of his final year in high school. Presently, he continues to live in the group home and now works in a sheltered work environment for persons with developmental disabilities. The residential and workshop staff have not adopted the communication alternative to dealing with his behavior. Major impediments to cooperation appear to be differences in philosophy and education of personnel at the school and other agencies, and a sense of competitiveness about which agency is best at dealing with specific individuals. The reported success at the school was viewed by the group home as "nonbehavioral," and, therefore, not valuable in the long-term objectives.

The first step in expanding and changing Jesse's communication system involves removing the barriers to interagency cooperation for Jesse and other students. Second, in terms of communication, the personnel at his living and work situations must learn and support Jesse's communication efforts. Third, his existing communication skills must be more easily read by persons in the various home, work, and community environments that he frequents. This means that his vocalizations and gestures must either be developed so that naive persons can understand his message or changed to an augmentative system of pictures or printed words.

ERNIE

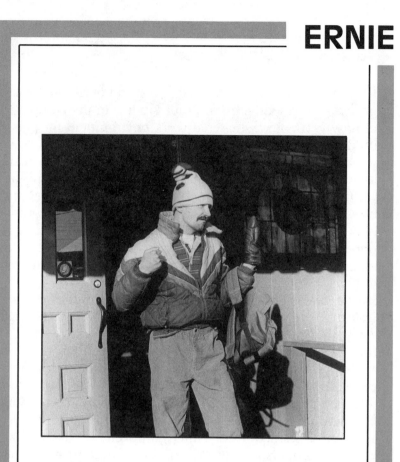

NAME: Ernie
AGE: 37 years
TEACHERS: Susan Purdy
Kathy Schenck
CONSULTANTS: Diane Baumgart
John VanWalleghem

SYSTEM

The system developed for Ernie was a 3 inch by 5 inch, three-ring binder system with one photo. The system fit in his back pants pocket and was used to purchase a beverage at a fast food restaurant. Later, a photo representing a restroom was added so he could inform people he was going to the restroom. The booklet was expanded further using line drawings. This increased his interactions throughout the day by helping others "recognize" a message after his initiations.

OVERVIEW

Ernie moved to an eight-person Intermediate Care Facility for the Mentally Retarded (ICF-MR) at the age of 37. Prior to this, he lived in a state institution for 32 years. In this new community, he attended a community-based life skills program during the day where he received instruction within restaurants, grocery stores, job sites, a bowling alley, the public library, and a classroom at the University of Idaho. He had resided in his new home and attended this day program for 6 months when the augmentative system assessment was initiated. His file listed him as having mental retardation in the severe to profound range. His developmental profile is discussed in the section that follows.

INFORMATION FROM AGENCY RECORDS

The information from Ernie's agency records includes his status in motor skills, vision, cognition, speech and language, and behavior.

211

Motor Skills

Ernie's fine motor skills included the use of the radial digital, scissors grasp, and pincer grasp (Cohen & Gross, 1979). These skills enabled Ernie to pick up small objects (e.g., coins from a table), hold small objects (e.g., insert coins into a vending machine), and turn pages of books and some magazines. Ernie walked using a wide gait and stiff, whole-leg movements. His balance was unsteady on grass and other uneven terrain. Climbing and descending stairs were performed using support and by placing both feet on each step. His development in these areas was at a 2-year level.

Vision

Ernie had functional vision with stabismus and hand-eye perception difficulties that were noted in past reports. No acuity problems requiring corrective lenses were noted in past reports.

Cognition

No specific information was in his file beyond Ernie's IQ level of severe and profound.

Speech and Language

Ernie's reports listed him as vocal, using the words "Hi" with hand gestures and "Ba" with an approximation of the sign bathroom and other gestures to indicate bathroom. Other vocalizations that Ernie used, with a variety of intonations, were noted as being incomprehensible.

Behavior

Past records noted that Ernie showed aggressive behavioral outbursts, as well as a social and likeable personality. Current staff noted that aggressive behaviors (e.g., hitting, breaking windows) occurred in new situations or in response to new tasks, and described the aggression as due to fear (i.e., excessive) of unknown situations. In familiar situations and routines, where demands were minimal, Ernie's personality was social and likeable.

ASSESSMENT FOR COMMUNICATION SYSTEM PLANNING

Prior to initiating further assessments, Ernie's teachers, group home supervisors, and his representative/advocate met to discuss his communication. At this meeting, it was decided that his gestures for "hi" and "bathroom" would continue to be accepted. It was also determined that sign language was not readily understood by most people and even his sign of 10 years (i.e., for bathroom) was difficult to discern, possibly because of his fine motor problems. A readily recognizable and portable system was requested since he spent most of his weekdays in the community and went on many outings with the group home staff. Ernie's representative strongly preferred the use of photos for his communication system. His teachers thought miniatures might be too difficult to locate and might limit expansion of the system. The decision was to use line drawings or photos and to place them in a small holder.

Prior to the design and implementation of the line drawing or photo system, a number of additional questions were raised. These questions, associated assessment procedures, and assessment results and conclusions are described below.

Question 1:   What Was Ernie's Level of Cognitive Development?

Ernie's previous history of institutionalization, observed difficulty in new situations, and lack of cognitive assessments in his file made it difficult to evaluate his cognitive level. His mental age was assumed to be a low estimate of his ability because of his lack of previous education and his institutionalization. Ernie's records indicated that he was untestable using standardized tests, and that attempts at tabletop cognitive assessments resulted in hitting, yelling, and throwing items. It was decided to collect information throughout a longer period using informal assessments.

Informal Assessments Informal assessments were completed throughout a 2-month interval, during familiar daily routines. Later, formal test situations were utilized. The assessment procedures used included partial and total visible and invisible displacement of favorite objects (e.g., tapes for the tape player); matching identical objects, pictures, and primary colors (e.g., coffee cups, silverware, plates, cans of soda and cups, coats, backpacks, hats, pencils, paper, coins); getting parts of objects to complete a task when some of the parts were missing (e.g., painting supplies, coffee pot, tape player, tapes, earphones, stapler, work papers); and two- and three-choice discrimination of objects, pictures, and colors given an exemplar (e.g., objects as above, the primary colors plus black).

Results Within daily routines, Ernie was able to locate tapes after invisible displacements, match objects to identical ones, and locate missing parts of objects that were needed with 100% accuracy. In test situations, he was noncompliant when tested for permanence. During other tests, he could locate parts with 100% accuracy and matched identical objects with 50% accuracy (chance level). Ernie was unable to match pictures or photos with either the actual object or the representation given one or two choices (accuracy ranged from 10% to 40%). When provided an exemplar, Ernie's accuracy was 57%, slightly higher than chance level. He was able to match the colors of red and black with 100% accuracy when given two to five piles of colored cards. All other cards were matched with an accuracy ranging between 20%–87%.

Conclusions An estimate of Ernie's cognitive level is within the 12–18 month range, Sensorimotor Stage V. In terms of communication, this stage is characterized by learning to achieve familiar items through new means, comprehending words in context, and performing actions when given simple directions accompanied by gestures and some content. These traits were characteristic of some of Ernie's behavior. His ability to match only the colors red and black may be due to past instruction with these colors. If color coding is used in his communication system, red and black will be used.

Question 2: What Pragmatic Intents Does He Exhibit within Familiar Settings and Routines? What Is His Receptive Vocabulary?

Assessment To assess pragmatics, Ernie was observed across daily and weekend schedules to determine how he might be using vocalizations, gestures, and other behaviors to communicate. He was usually observed by one of his teachers or a practicum student. Probes, where two observers collected information, were conducted on three different days for 2 hours each day in order to collect interrater reliability. Samples of the data collected are contained in Figure 8.1 (see Appendix A.8 for a blank form).

The assessment of receptive vocabulary was conducted in structured testing situations and through observations during routines. Ernie was tested on words for items he enjoyed using, including: dominoes, coat, magazine, timer, tape recorder, black and red cards (i.e., a teacher-made card game), cup, facial tissue, money, Perfection (i.e., a commercial game), coffee pot, sponge, and soda. Within the context or routines where these items were typically used, Ernie was given the request, "Show me," or, "Ernie, get the _____."

Results Ernie was able to perform the requested actions within the natural routines for six items at 100% accuracy when given the request and gesture toward the general location of the item. He was not able to comply with requests for a specific item when the objects were out of the context in which they were typically used.

The result of the receptive vocabulary assessments were interpreted to mean that Ernie's receptive vocabulary was limited and that context and routines were necessary to help him comprehend verbal speech. Such receptive vocabulary should be utilized to enhance comprehension. A communication system should be introduced and taught to Ernie within the con-

Pragmatic Intent Observation Data

Name: Ernie   Date: March 10, 1985   Observer: K.S.

Categories	Location	Example of activity and interpretation (write up third example observed)	Other comments
1. Makes a request; asks a question	University classroom	Vocalization with question intonation and pointing to object or place Example: Brought a can of soda to teacher, pointed to unopened top, and vocalized with question intonation. Interpretation (100% interrater reliability) was, "Help me?"	
	University classroom, Bowling alley, and Restaurant	Example: Says, "Ba" with question intonation and grasps self below belt. Interpretation (100% interrater reliability) was, "May I go to the bathroom?"	
	Mall cafeteria	Example: Pointed to food in cafeteria line and vocalized without question intonation. When given food, he smiled. Interpretation (100% interrater reliability) was, "I want that."	
2. Gives an answer or responds to a question or request	University classroom	Consistently uses vocalization "No" and gestures and intonation emphasizing negation. Example: Says, "No, No!" and grabs materials back when another adult took away cards he was using. Interpretation was, "No, don't do that!"	
	Breakroom	Example: Says, "No!" and stomps feet when teacher requested him to get a magazine during break.	Group home staff reported similar behavior. Doesn't like magazines.
	University classroom	Example: Says, "No!" waits, and goes to cupboard to get a card game when attendant says, "Ernie, get the cards from the cupboard." Interpretation was, "O.K., I heard you."	Ernie says, "No," but often just says it because it's a word. Intonation helps separate meaning, "No," from saying something.

3. Describes events or aspects of the environment	Public library and Total Textiles	Does so with vocalization and gestures. Example: Clapped hands and smiled when finished work at community job sites. Interpretation was, "I'm pleased, I'm finished!"	Not observed as frequently as above two categories.
	Skipper's Restaurant	Example: Pointed to van when 1/2 block away and vocalized "Da!, Da!" Smiled when staff pointed to van too and said, "The van is here, yes, Ernie!" Interpretation was, "Look! Here's our (my) van!"	
4. Expresses facts, beliefs, attitudes, or emotions	University classroom	Does so with hand and facial gestures. Example: Stomps feet, hits, and looks scared when he was requested to go down steep outdoor steps. Interpretation was, "I'm scared!"	
	Group home	Example: Shook finger at roommate and looked mad and vocalized sounds loudly. Interpretation was, "I'm mad at you!"	Staff report this occurs about once a week.
5. Attempts to, and does establish or maintain interpersonal contact or interaction	Total Textiles	Does so with verbal, "Hi!" and gestures. Example: Walks into worksite and hugs supervisor. Interpretation was, "Hi, so nice to see you!"	
	Community	Example: Says, "Hi!" to strangers as they walk past him as he walks to work. Example: Taps arm of staff and says, "Hi!" Interpretation was, "Let's talk!"	People typically smile and return greetings.
6. Attempts to entertain or tease others		No evidence observed	

Figure 8.1. Sample of Pragmatic Intent Observation Data collected on Ernie.

text of natural routines within his schedule and not as a tabletop repeated trials task.

Conclusions The pragmatic assessment was interpreted to mean that Ernie used a variety of gestures and vocal intonations to communicate and that he used all pragmatic categories except for teasing and joking. The most frequent communication initiations, in order of highest frequency of occurrence, were making requests and asking questions; giving answers, responding to questions and requests (especially to indicate "no"); attempting, establishing, or maintaining interpersonal contact or interactions; and expressing facts, beliefs, attitudes, or emotions (especially emotions). A nonverbal system should utilize these strengths and include at least some of these intents. A system to initiate requests in a social context was recommended. This would incorporate both his most frequent intent (i.e., requests) and his attempts to interact with others. Saying, "No," and being able to escape or terminate something should also be a communicative "word" on his system.

Question 3: What Visual Tracking and Scanning Skills Could He Use When Given Several Objects or Pictures?

Assessments Ernie was requested to look at vertical and horizontal arrays of objects and pictures both within the routine of his day and in testing situations. The arrays were presented at eye level, above eye level, and below eye level. The objects were those often used during his activities, plus others, if needed, to produce an array of two or three. An example of an assessment during a daily routine consisted of placing his backpack on a table along with another person's schedule book and wallet. He was then asked to get his backpack.

Results Ernie did not track or scan objects or pictures in vertical arrays at his midline, to the left or right of midline, or above eye level position. When objects or pictures were presented at and below eye level, Ernie scanned horizontal arrays of two or three objects or pictures when given a request and a pointing gesture. He was not able to track the pointing gesture or scan horizontal arrays that were presented above eye level.

Conclusions The items in the communication system should be in a horizontal array at or below eye level. Ernie may need assistance with scanning two or more representations. Initially, the presentation should consist of one item to avoid the additional scanning skills that are not currently in his repertoire.

Question 4: What Motor Responses Could Ernie Reliably Use to Attract Attention to His Nonverbal Messages or to Make a Selection?

Assessment Ernie was requested to point to various favorite small items on a table prior to receiving them. He was able to point with his index finger when given a model and a request to do so; however, he used a whole hand touch when pointing spontaneously. Ernie was also assessed on his ability to cross midline with either hand and on his preferred hand use. Items that he typically liked were placed on a table before him in a horizontal array in such a manner that he would have to cross midline to obtain one of them (e.g., a straw and a container of soda with a lid, a cup and a pot of coffee).

Results Ernie typically used his left hand to obtain items, but switched to his right hand to obtain an object rather than cross midline to use his left hand. If both objects were to the left of midline, Ernie used his left hand to obtain them. If both objects were to the right of midline, he used his right hand.

Conclusion Ernie's teachers felt that he could use a pointing response reliably and that he could use an index-finger point if requested specifically to do so. Because a whole hand response can block the picture or line drawing from the receiver's view, a finger point was recommended. He may need a verbal or modeled cue of the required response. A symbol placed on each representation was recommended as a reminder of where and how to point. A red Bliss symbol for "Want" was placed on each photo as a reminder of where to point.

In addition, the hand preference and midline assessments were interpreted to indicate that he preferred to use his left hand but crossing midline made that difficult. The horizontal array at or below eye level should be positioned so that he could access it with his left hand without having to cross midline.

Summary of Results Used in Selecting a System

Ernie appears to be functioning within Sensorimotor Stage V. This would indicate that he would have difficulty perceiving representations (e.g., pictures, photos, line drawings) as symbols of the actual object. However, due to Ernie's age, the resulting social stigma associated with carrying the real object, the extensive amount of walking that he does to work and other community sites, and the preferences of his teachers, group home supervisors, and representative/advocate, photos with high visual representations of objects were selected for Ernie's communication system.

The pragmatic assessments and receptive vocabulary data indicate that making requests for objects and initiating a variety of types of interactions with others were the highest frequency communicative intents observed. Thus, requests for favorite items (e.g., soda, Perfection, bathroom) were selected as initial vocabulary words to be used as the need arose at a restaurant, breakroom at a worksite, the group home, and the day activity center. Soda was selected as the starting vocabulary word because Ernie had frequent opportunities to request this item daily. A photo for bathroom was added to his wallet later but did not replace his verbalization, "Ba." The photo was used in conjunction with the verbalization to ensure his request was consistently understood. The format selected was one photo in a plastic sleeve within a 3 inch by 5 inch, three-ring binder. The binder was placed in his left back pocket for easy access and portability. The word or phrase was written on each photo card to enhance the specific message. Ernie is shown using his communication system in Figure 8.2.

Figure 8.2. Ernie using his system at Skipper's Restaurant.

Practice sessions (i.e., simulations) for using the communication system were scheduled three times a week in addition to the naturally occurring occasions that are listed above. The goals for the system were:

1. To provide Ernie with a formal system of communication that would readily be used and comprehended with different people, situations, and environments
2. To provide him with a highly portable and socially acceptable system for use in the community
3. To provide a method with which Ernie could initiate requests and be readily understood
4. To provide a method that could be readily expanded and revised

EFFECTIVENESS OF THE SYSTEM

Data were collected on Ernie's use of the system to order a beverage at the local Skipper's Restaurant. The restaurant se-

lected for instruction was two blocks from a prevocational instruction site, seven blocks from the university classroom, and
three blocks from the grocery where he shopped. It was also
typical of most of the fast food restaurants in the town (i.e., the

Form for Ordering and Paying for a Beverage at a Fast Food Restaurant

Name: Ernie   Date: 5–11

Observer: John   Site: Skipper's Restaurant

Objective: Given a verbal cue, "Ernie, get your communication book out"; assistance to open to the correct page; and the cue, "Go ahead and order," Ernie will
perform the activity steps 1–27 once, independently. He will do this three times a week
for two consecutive weeks.

Activities	Date 5–11
1. Moves to counter/order area	V
2. When cashier is ready, looks at cashier	+
3. Opens communication book	+
4. Places book on counter	FA
5. Turns picture right side up if necessary	G
6. Turns book to face cashier if necessary	G
7. Points to picture so cashier can see	FA
8. Waits for cashier to acknowledge order	+
9. Opens wallet	FA
10. Reaches into billfold section	PP
11. Takes out a dollar bill	PP
12. Hands money to cashier	M
13. Puts open wallet on counter	G
14. Opens coin purse flap	PP
15. Hooks index finger of left hand in coin purse in order to hold open	PP
16. Accepts change from cashier with right hand	+
17. Puts change in purse section	PP
18. Closes flap of coin purse	M
19. Closes wallet	G
20. Picks up wallet	G
21. Picks up communication book	V
22. Stays at counter till order is complete	V
23. Receives/picks up beverage	+
24. Moves away from order area	V
25. Carries drink to table, no drinking	V
26. Moves to table	V
27. Sits in chair	V

Code key: + = independent; V = verbal; G = gestural; M = model; FA = full
assistance; PP = physical prompt (above elbow); − = not accomplished even with
assistance.

Figure 8.3.   Sample data on Ernie, used for ordering and paying for a beverage at a fast food restaurant.

ordering and payment routines were similar as confirmed by staff observations of 30 restaurants). In addition to Skipper's Restaurant, some ordering was done at an Arby's and Zip's Restaurants to probe for generalization.

Sample data on Ernie's use of the system is presented in Figure 8.3 (see Appendix A.11 for a blank form). A summary of his progress data for ordering is contained in Figure 8.4. He also learned to pay for his order, walk to a booth, drink his beverage with others, and leave. These data are not summarized here; however, he did master these activities as well as walking to each restaurant with minimal supervision.

Ernie met criterion on the objectives of ordering and paying for a beverage at Skipper's 6 months after instruction was

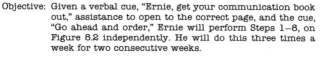

Name: *Ernie*
Objective: Given a verbal cue, "Ernie, get your communication book out," assistance to open to the correct page, and the cue, "Go ahead and order," Ernie will perform Steps 1–8, on Figure 8.2 independently. He will do this three times a week for two consecutive weeks.

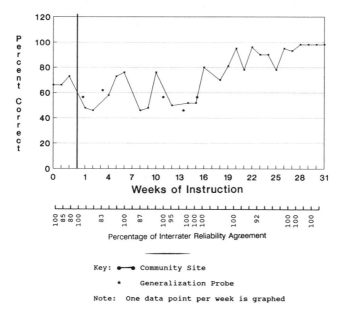

Figure 8.4. Summary of progress data on Ernie, used for ordering at a fast food restaurant.

initiated. The ordering segment was mastered sooner than the payment segment. From Figure 8.3, Step 6, "Turning the book to face the cashier," and Steps 13–15, manipulating his wallet to pay, gave him the most difficulty. These steps were practiced at the university classroom to give him more experience using the necessary skills.

SUGGESTIONS FOR EXPANDING OR CHANGING THE SYSTEM

The photo wallet system worked well for Ernie and the question of how to expand the system was discussed. The skills needed to turn pages and to select a referent for various interactions were not skills the staff thought Ernie could acquire. At the same time, Ernie was having difficulty ordering because he continued to "talk" after he received his beverage rather than moving aside so other customers could order. It appeared that Ernie wanted to interact more! The teachers reviewed Ernie's daily schedule and identified the routines where he could interact with others or have "more to say" during interactions. They decided that since Ernie was always with a teacher or group home supervisor, and since he liked using his system, a new expanded system would be made. The new system was a 3 inch by 5 inch three-ring binder for mealtimes, with many line drawings. Tabs with environments listed on them were used to divide the book into sections. Each section had line drawings that represented vocabulary that was typically used in interactions in each environment. Prior to entering an environment or engaging in an activity, the book was opened to the correct page for Ernie and he interacted with a variety of people using the new system. For instance, at a cafeteria, his book was opened for him so he could answer to "Large or small salad?," "Dressing?," and, "Is this to go or stay?" At his job site, Ernie could respond to, "Want a Coke?", initiate greetings, and comment on his choice of beverage in the breakroom. His inappropriate "talking" decreased, although he continued to verbalize while walking to and from environments,

Figure 8.5. Ernie's expanded system.

viewed as acceptable for Ernie. This expanded system is shown in Figure 8.5.

SUMMARY

Ernie was given a system of photos and, subsequently, line drawings that were not recognizable as referents of objects or events by him and that some would say was a system that was too difficult for him based on his developmental level. Ernie did, however, learn to use this system to bring more communication partners into his routines. Because of his age, his motivation to interact, and the need for others to readily comprehend his initiations and responses, the social significance of the system was thought to outweigh Ernie's cognitive inability to readily match pictures with their referents.

Data acquired 2 years after intervention was initiated indicated that Ernie was using his photo system to order beverages at a variety of community functions including restaurants, church functions, and concession stands at parks and sporting

events. The 3 inch by 5 inch three-ring binder with line drawings was discontinued. Ernie's placement during the day was
changed to a segregated day activity program and the expanded system was not felt to be necessary. It is important to
note that this change of placement was a policy decision and
not a result of his behavior or lack of behavior.

REFERENCES

Alberto, P.A., & Troutman, A.C. (1986). *Applied behavior analysis for teachers* (2nd ed.). Columbus, OH: Charles E. Merrill.

Alpern, G., Boll, T., & Shearer, M. (1984). *Developmental Profile II*. Los Angeles: Western Psychological Services.

Batshaw, M.L., & Perret, Y.M. (1986). *Children with handicaps: A medical primer* (2nd ed.). Baltimore: Paul H. Brookes Publishing Co.

Bayley, N. (1969). *Bayley Scales of Infant Development*. Atlanta: The Psychological Corporation.

Blackman, J.A. (Ed.). (1984). *Medical aspects of developmental disabilities in children—birth to three* (rev. 1st ed.). Rockville, MD: Aspen Publishers Inc.

Bloom, L., & Lahey, M. (1978). *Language development and language disorders*. New York: John Wiley & Sons.

Brown, L., Branston, M.B., Hamre-Nietupski, S., Pumpian, I., Certo, N., & Gruenewald, L. (1979). A strategy for developing chronological age-appropriate and functional curricular content for severely handicapped adolescents and young adults. *Journal of Special Education, 13,* 81–90.

Brown, L., Branston-McLean, M., Baumgart, D., Vincent, L., Falvey, M., & Schroeder, J. (1979). Using the characteristics of current and subsequent least restrictive environments in the development of curricular content for the severely handicapped students. *AAESPH Review, 4,* 407–424.

Bruner, J. (1974/1975). From communication to language: A psychological perspective. *Cognition, 3,* 255–287.

Carr, E.G., & Durand, V.M. (1985). Reducing behavior problems through functional communication training. *Journal of Applied Behavior Analysis, 18,* 111–126.

Carrow, E. (1973). *Test for Auditory Comprehension of Language*. Austin, TX: Learning Concepts.

Cohen, M.A., & Gross, P.J. (1979). *The developmental resource: Behav-*

ioral sequencing for assessment and program planning (Vols. 1–2). New York: Grune & Stratton.

Donnellan, A.M., Mirenda, P., Mesarsos, R.A., & Fassbender, L.L. (1984). Analyzing the communicative functions of aberrant behavior. *Journal of the Association for Persons with Severe Handicaps, 9,* 201–212.

Dore, J. (1974). A pragmatic description of early language development. *Journal of Psycholinguistic Research, 4,* 343–350.

Dore, J. (1975). Holophrases, speech acts, and language universals. *Journal of Child Language, 2*(1), 21–40.

Dorland's Illustrated Medical Dictionary. (1981). Philadelphia: W.B. Saunders.

Duchan, J. (1983). Autistic children are noninteractive: Or so we say. *Seminars in Speech and Language, 4*(1), 53–62.

Dunn, L.M. (1965). *Peabody Picture Vocabulary Test.* Circle Pines, MN: American Guidance Service.

Durand, V.M., & Carr, E.G. (1987). Social influences on "self-stimulatory" behavior: Analysis and treatment application. *Journal of Applied Behavior Analysis, 20,* 119–132.

Durand, V.M., & Crimmins, D.B. (1988). Identifying the variables maintaining self-injurious behavior. *Journal of Autism and Developmental Disorders, 18,* 99–117.

Erhardt, R.P. (1986). *Erhardt Developmental Vision Assessment.* Fargo, ND: Author. (Available from R.P. Erhardt, 2109 Third St., North, Fargo, ND 58102)

Evans, I.M., & Meyer, L.H. (1985). *An educative approach to behavior problems: A practical decision model for interventions with severely handicapped learners.* Baltimore: Paul H. Brookes Publishing Co.

Falvey, M., Brown, L., Lyon, S., Baumgart, D., & Schroeder, J. (1980). Strategies for using cues and correction procedures. In W. Sailor, B. Wilcox, & L. Brown (Eds.), *Methods of instruction for severely handicapped students* (pp. 109–133). Baltimore: Paul H. Brookes Publishing Co.

Filler, J., Baumgart, D., & Askvig, B. (1989). Mainstreaming young children with disabilities. In W. Sailor, J. Anderson, K.F. Doering, J. Filler, L. Goetz, & A. Halvorsen. *The comprehensive local school: Regular education for all students with disabilities.* Baltimore: Paul H. Brookes Publishing Co.

Gadow, K.D. (1986). *Children on medication* (Vols. 1–2). San Diego: College-Hill Press.

Hagberg, B., Aicardi, J., Dias, K., & Ramos, O. (1983). A progressive syndrome of autism, dementia, ataxia, and loss of purposeful hand use in girls: Rett's syndrome: Report of 35 cases. *Annals of Neurology, 14,* 471–479.

Halle, J. (1985). Arranging the natural environment to occasions language: Giving severely language-delayed children reasons to communicate. *Seminars in Speech and Language, 5,* 185–196.

Harding, C. (1984). Acting with intention: A framework for examining the development of the intention to communicate. In L. Feagans, C. Garvey, & R. Golinkoff (Eds.), *The origins and growth of communication.* Norwood, NJ: Ablex Publishing.

Haslam, R.H., & Valletutti, P.J. (1985). *Medical problems in the classroom: The teacher's role in diagnosis and management.* Austin, TX: PRO-ED.

Holvoet, J.F., & Helmstetter, E. (1989). *Medical problems of students with special needs: A guide for educators.* Boston: College-Hill Press.

Maslow, A.H. (1968). *Toward a psychology of being.* Princeton, NJ: Van Nostrand.

McCarney, S.B. (1983). *Adaptive Behavior Evaluation Scale.* Columbia, MO: Hawthorne Educational Services.

McDonald, J. (1985). Language through conversation. In S. Warren & A. Rogers-Warren (Eds.), *Teaching functional language* (pp. 89–122). Baltimore: University Park Press.

McLean, J., & Snyder-McLean, L. (1978). *A transactional approach to early language training.* Columbus, OH: Charles E. Merrill.

Meyer, L.H., & Evans, I.M. (1989). *Nonaversive intervention for behavior problems: A manual for home and community.* Baltimore: Paul H. Brookes Publishing Co.

Musselwhite, C.R., & St. Louis, K.W. (1982). *Communication programming for the severely handicapped: Vocal and non-vocal strategies.* San Diego: College-Hill Press.

Pecyna, P.M., & Sommers, R.K. (1985). Testing the receptive language skills of severely handicapped children. *Language, Speech, and Hearing Services in Schools, 16*(1), 41–52.

Rice, M. (1984). Cognitive aspects of communicative development. In R. Schiefelbusch & J. Pickar (Eds.), *The acquisition of communicative competence* (pp. 141–189). Baltimore: University Park Press.

Sailor, W., & Mix, B.J. (1975). *The TARC Assessment System.* Lawrence, KS: H & H Enterprises.

Scheuerman, N., Baumgart, D., Sipsma, K., & Brown, L. (1976). Toward the development of a curriculum for teaching non-verbal communication skills to severely handicapped students: Teaching tracking, scanning and selection skills. In L. Brown, N. Scheuerman, & T. Crowner (Eds.), *Madison's alternative to zero exclusion: Toward an integrated therapy model for teaching motor, tracking and scanning skills to severely handicapped students* (pp. 71–248). Madison, WI: Madison Public Schools and University of Wisconsin-Madison.

Schuler, A.L. (1980). Aspects of cognition. In W.H. Fay & A.L. Schuler (Eds.), *Emerging language in autistic children* (pp. 113–136). Baltimore: University Park Press.

Schuler, A.L., Peck, C.A., Willard, C., & Theimer, K. (1989). Assessment of communicative means and functions through interview: Assessing the communicative capabilities of individuals with limited language. *Seminars in Speech and Language, 10*, 51–62.

Schuler, A.L., & Prizant, B.M. (1987). Facilitating communication: Prelanguage approaches. In D.J. Cohen & A.M. Donnellan (Eds.), *Handbook of autism and pervasive developmental disorders*. Silver Spring, MD: V.H. Winston & Sons.

Silverman, F.H. (1980). *Communication for the speechless*. Englewood Cliffs, NJ: Prentice-Hall.

Silverman, F.H. (1989). *Communication for the speechless*. Engelwood Cliffs, NJ: Prentice-Hall.

Snow, C. (1972). Mother's speech to children learning language. *Child Development, 43*, 549–566.

Sparrow, S.S., Balla, D.A., & Cicchetti, D.V. (1984). *Vineland Adaptive Behavior Scales (Interview Edition, Expanded Form)*. Circle Pines, MN: American Guidance Service.

Stonestreet, R., Augustine, R., & Johnson, J. (1986, October). *Communication assessment for 0–3-year-olds*. Unpublished manuscript.

Sugarman, S. (1984). The development of preverbal communication. In R. Schiefelbusch & J. Pickar (Eds.), *The acquisition of communicative competence*. Baltimore: University Park Press.

Tawney, J.W., & Gast, D.L. (1984). *Single subject research in special education*. Columbus, OH: Charles E. Merrill.

Tingey, C. (1989). *Implementing early intervention*. Baltimore: Paul H. Brookes Publishing Co.

Wetherby, A., Cain, D., Yonclas, D., & Walker, V. (1988). Analysis of intentional communication of normal children from the prelinguistic to the multi-word stage. *Journal of Speech and Hearing Research, 31*, 240–252.

Wetherby, A.M., & Prizant, B.M. (1989). The expression of communicative intent: Assessment guidelines. *Seminars in Speech and Language, 10,* 77–90.

Wolfensberger, W. (1972). *The principle of normalization in human services.* Toronto, Canada: National Institute on Mental Retardation.

REFERENCES

APPENDIX

Communication Interview

Cue Questions:	Crying	Aggression	Tantrums/self-injury	Passive gaze	Proximity	Pulling other's hands	Touching/moving other's face	Grabs/reaches	Enactment	Removes self/walks away	Vocalization/noise	Active gaze	Gives object	Gestures/pointing	Facial expression	Shakes "no"/nods "yes"	Intonation	Inapproppriate echolalia	Appropriate echolalia	One-word speech	One-word signs	Complex speech	Complex signs
1. Requests for affection/interaction: WHAT IF S WANTS																							
Adult to sit near?																							
Peer to sit near?																							
Nonhandicapped peer to sit near?																							
Adult to look at him or her?																							
Adult to tickle him or her?																							
To cuddle or embrace?																							
To sit on adult's lap?																							
Other:																							
2. Requests for adult action: WHAT IF S WANTS																							
Help with dressing?																							
To be read a book?																							

To play ball/a game?																
To go outside/to store?																
Other:																
3. Requests for object, food, or things: WHAT IF S WANTS																
An object out of reach?																
A door/container opened?																
A favorite food?																
Music/radio/television?																
Keys/toy/book?																
Other:																
4. Protest: WHAT IF																
Common routine is dropped?																
Favorite toy/food taken away?																
Taken for ride without desire?																
Adult terminates interaction?																
Required to do something he or she doesn't want to do?																
Other:																
5. Declaration/comment: WHAT IF S WANTS																
To show you something?																
You to look at something?																
Other:																

From Schuler, A. L., Peck, C. A., Willard, C., & Theimer, K. (1989). Assessment of communicative means and functions through interview: Assessing the communicative capabilities of individuals with limited language. *Seminars in Speech and Language, 10,* 54; copyright © 1989 by Thieme Medical Publishers, Inc.; reprinted by permission.

Anecdotal Recording

Student: _____ Teacher: _____ Observer: _____
Date: _____ Begin time: _____ End time: _____
Locations: _____
Behavior: _____

Time	Antecedent	Behavior	Consequence

Grid for Expanding Communication Systems

Aspects	Existing[a]	New[b]
Behavioral Form	(Describe)	
Vocal		
Verbal		
Gestural		
Gaze		
Other:		
Symbolic form	(Describe appearance and/or list)	
Real objects		
Replicas		
Miniatures		
Photos		
Pictures		
Other:		
Function of signal	(Describe specific function in each category[c])	
Behavioral regulation		
Social interaction		
Joint activity		
Communication partner	(List names and familiarity with system user)	
Person: Familiar/ unfamiliar		
Environment/activity/context	(List by category)	
Daily		
Weekly		
Monthly		
Other:		
Assistance	(Describe type)	
Natural cues/prompts		
Frequency		
Instructional cues/prompts		
Frequency		

[a]Existing = currently used.
[b]New = changed.
[c]See Wetherby and Prizant (1989)

Visual Tracking Data Sheet

Name:_____   Date:_____

Observer:_____   Materials Used:_____

Instructions: Using objects that the individual will readily watch, begin at the appropriate reference point (indicated by the letters and boxes) and move the object along the designated visual plane. Watch the individual's eyes during tracking and indicate whether the tracking was continuous or interrupted. Also record if there were any indications of nystagmus or strabismus.

Horizontal, above eye level: (A to B and B to A)_____ Continuous _____ Interrupted

Horizontal, at eye level: (C to D and D to C) _____ Continuous _____ Interrupted

Horizontal, below eye level: (E to F and F to E) _____ Continuous _____ Interrupted

Vertical (at midline): (G to H and H to G) _____ Continuous _____ Interrupted

Diagonal: (A to F and F to A) _____ Continuous _____ Interrupted

Diagonal: (B to E and E to B) _____ Continuous _____ Interrupted

Nystagmus (bouncing eyes): _____ Right _____ Left _____ Both

Strabismus (eyes turn in/out): _____ Right _____ Left _____ Both

Comments:

Visual Scanning Checklist

Name: _____   Date: _____

Observer: _____

1. Where does the student begin his or her visual search?
   ____ Top left   ____ Center   ____ Top right
   ____ Bottom left   ____ Bottom right

2. What is his or her pattern of scanning?
   ____ Left to right   ____ Top to bottom   ____ Random pattern
   ____ Right to left   ____ Bottom to top   ____ No discernible pattern

3. Does the student scan the entire set of materials? ____ Yes   ____ No
   If no, which area does he or she not scan? _____

4. Does the student maintain his or her attention to scanning task?
   ____ Yes   ____ No
   For how long? _____

5. Can the student quickly (e.g., less than 10 seconds) locate the requested symbol
   when presented with:
   3 items ____ Yes   ____ No   6 items ____ Yes   ____ No
   4 items ____ Yes   ____ No   8 items ____ Yes   ____ No
                 ____ items ____ Yes   ____ No

6. How does the student select the appropriate item?
   ____ Maintains gaze   ____ Names item   ____ Vocalizes
   ____ Points to item   ____ Picks up item   ____ Shows excitement
   ____ Other (specify) _____

7. What type of prompts are helpful in assisting the student to scan?
   ____ Pointing by student   ____ Physically turning the student's head
   ____ Pointing by teacher   ____ Color cues
   ____ Other (specify) _____

Data Sheet for Assessing Hand Preference

Date:_____ Observer:_____

Name:_____ Time:_____

Materials used: _____

Which hand is used to pick up objects when the object is placed in the following locations in relation to the body? Put an X in the blank which describes the hand used.

Left front   Right front

                              Middle

Left side   Right side

                              Student
                              is here
                          facing forward

Sitting at table:

	L hand		R hand	
Left front:	L hand	___	R hand	___
Left side:	L hand	___	R hand	___
Middle:	L hand	___	R hand	___
Right front:	L hand	___	R hand	___
Right side:	L hand	___	R hand	___

Standing:

	L hand		R hand	
Left front:	L hand	___	R hand	___
Left side:	L hand	___	R hand	___
Middle:	L hand	___	R hand	___
Right front:	L hand	___	R hand	___
Right side:	L hand	___	R hand	___

A.7

Form and Use Assessment Sheet

Name of client: _____

Observer: _____

Date: _____

Context	Partner	Child signal	Partner response	Discourse function[a]	Pragmatic function[b]

[a]Discourse functions served by the child's signal: initiate, maintain, terminate, or repair conversation.

[b]Pragmatic functions of the child's signal: request object or action, protest, request social routine, greeting, showing off, calling, request permission, acknowledgment, comment, request information, clarification (see Wetherby and Prizant [1989] or Chapter Two for definitions).

241

Pragmatic Intent Observation Data

Name: _____   Date: _____   Observer: _____

Categories	Location/time/frequency	Example of activity and interpretation (write up third example observed)	Other comments
1. Makes a request; asks a question			
2. Gives an answer or responds to a question or request			
3. Describes events or aspects of the environment			
4. Expresses facts, beliefs, attitudes, or emotions			
5. Attempts to, and does establish or maintain interpersonal contact or interaction			
6. Attempts to entertain or tease others			

Basic Receptive Language Assessment Form

Name: _____   Date: _____   Observer: _____

Instructions: Present two objects to the student. Name one of the objects and ask the student to point to it, look at it, or use it (any of these responses is acceptable). Place an "X" in the appropriate column for the student's response. Compare at least 10 trials, varying the objects and the position of their presentation.

Objects presented	Object requested	Student's response	
		Correct	Incorrect

Comments:

Form for Collecting Procedural Data on Use of a System

Name: _____   Date: _____

Observer: _____   Time of day: A.M./P.M.

System activity	Goes to system	Gets object/symbol	Goes to activity
1.			
2.			
3.			
4.			
5.			
6.			
7.			
8.			
9.			
10.			

Key: I = Independent; V = Verbal prompt; G = Gestural prompt; OH = Orients head; P = Physical assistance.

Comments:

Form for Ordering and Paying for a Beverage at a Fast Food Restaurant

Name: _____ Date: _____
Observer: _____ Site: _____
Objective: _____
_____
_____
_____

Activities	Date

1. Moves to counter/order area
2. When cashier is ready, looks at cashier
3. Opens communication book
4. Places book on counter
5. Turns picture right side up if necessary
6. Turns book to face cashier if necessary
7. Points to picture so cashier can see
8. Waits for cashier to acknowledge order
9. Opens wallet
10. Reaches into billfold section
11. Takes out a dollar bill
12. Hands money to cashier
13. Puts open wallet on counter
14. Opens coin purse flap
15. Hooks index finger of left hand in coin purse in order to hold open
16. Accepts change from cashier with right hand
17. Puts change in purse section
18. Closes flap of coin purse
19. Closes wallet
20. Picks up wallet
21. Picks up communication book
22. Stays at counter till order is complete
23. Receives/picks up beverage
24. Moves away from order area
25. Carries drink to table, no drinking
26. Moves to table
27. Sits in chair

Code key: + = independent; V = verbal; G = gestural; M = model; FA = full assistance; PP = physical prompt (above elbow); − = not accomplished even with assistance.

INDEX